ABUNDANCE MAGIC

by

Katherine Tack

A BOOK ABOUT MONEY MAGIC

ISBN: 978-1-086971415 (Paperback)

Any references to historical events, real people, or real places are used fictitiously. Names, characters, and places are products of the author's imagination.

Front cover image by Katherine Tack.
Book design by Katherine Tack.

Printed by Amazon, in the United Kingdom.

First printing edition 2019.

Brand Magic Media Ltd
21 Blisworth Mill
Northamptonshire
NN7 3RZ

www.brand-magic.co.uk

FOREWORD

It is my pleasure, dear reader to provide a foreword to this book and 'money insight' oracle card deck by Katherine Tack. I have known Katherine, both as a friend, and as a trusted business colleague for nearly a decade. It's been amazing and interesting to see how our life path's have been inter-twined over the course of those years. And it's been a significant, as well as an enjoyable and fruitful relationship for both of us.

In fact, Activate Your Magic, the coaching program that re-ignited Katherine's desire to paint and write this book and create the 'money insights' system, would probably never have come about if I had not first received her help. Firstly, Katherine has provided all the beautiful branding and images for every launch of the 'Activate Your Magic' program. But going back even further than that, it was also Katherine's conviction that I MUST attend a certain energy healing workshop in London, that put me firmly on my current path. It's a path that allows me to enable talented, sensitive and creative people like Katherine to reconnect to their intuition and their creative gifts.

And it's one, I am very grateful to Katherine for helping me to find.

I have no doubt whatsoever that as you work through the proven systematic approach that Katherine shares here, to help you increase your abundance, that you'll also be inspired and influenced by some of Katherine's outstanding qualities.

For example, her ability to pick up the ball and run with it until she sees a project through to its successful completion. It's exactly this quality that makes Katherine the ideal teacher to help you wrestle your outdated abundance blocks and limiting beliefs to the ground. And she'll then inspire you to replace them with practical habits that really reward you and enable you to create the prosperity that you deserve.

There's also a deep wisdom and intelligence in this work that I'd like to draw your attention to. It's one that has its roots in the traditional teachings of the Native Americans. In this book Katherine skillfully draws on this body of teachings to remind us to pay attention to the animals around us and observe the patterns in which they behave.

Using Katherine's insightful text and her inspiring artwork, we are reminded that each animal has a simple, but important lesson to share with us.

Katherine also reminds us that we can draw on the strength and superpower that each of the animals represents as well. And finally, for those to whom it may seem strange, or selfish to spend time focusing on your own abundance, when everything in our world seems so unstable, I would like to encourage you to trust Katherine's intuition in sharing her system with you now.

Granted the times we live in are deeply unsettling. But breaking away from the old patterns that keep us in survival mode and instead, learning how to create our own financial freedom is part of the wider solution as well.

It's an essential skill that frees up more of our energy and time so that we can contribute more of ourselves and more of the gifts we have come to share with the people in our lives.

Estelle Gillingham, PhD
Author of "Be Who You Came To Be" and Creator of Activate Your Magic

About the Author:

Katherine Tack can usually be found running her branding business, 'Brand Magic', or painting a picture. Most probably a portrait of an animal and most probably abstract in nature.

Katherine learned to meditate at a young age and has always been spiritual. She attended many spiritual workshops and courses before crafting her own unique guided meditations.

Writing a book was always on her bucket list, and eventually, 'Abundance Magic', was born.

When not completely covered in paint and totally absorbed in the throws of a creative outlet, Katherine loves cooking, bakes very badly, enjoys rambling around the English countryside, and otherwise spends far too much time at her computer.

She lives in England, with her husband and family.

5% of all proceeds from this book
go to animal charities around the world.
www.abundance-magic.co.uk/payingitforward

CONTENTS

MAIN CHAPTERS	PAGE	ANIMAL CHAPTERS	PAGE
PREFACE	1	Bears	151
Getting Started	6	Butterfly	223
How It Works	110	Cheetah	173
1. Instincts	9	Cow	285
2. Self-Respect	23	Crab	256
3. Forgiveness	31	Crocodile	205
4. Self-Sabotage	40	Deer	246
5. Acknowledge	47	Dog	141
6. Symbols	57	Dragonfly	200
7. De Cluttering	67	Eagle	313
8. Visualisation	73	Elephant	183
9. Alternatives	83	Fish	178
10. Responsibility	87	Flamingo	291
11. Truth	91	Fox	219
		Frog	262
		Geese	234
		Goat	305
		Giraffe	229
		Hippopotamus	279
		Honey Bee	187
		Horse	213
		Kingfisher	241
		Monkey	133
		Mouse or Rat	118
		Ostrich	165
		Orangutan	297
		Owl	193
		Peacock	160
		Rabbit	252
		Ram	275
		Squirrel	147
		Tiger	123
		Turtle	209
		Warthog	320
		Worms	129
		Zebra	268

This book is dedicated to my husband.
Without his love and support,
this book would still be hibernating.

This book and money making card system was
inspired by the sensitive souls of the world who
give so much without even knowing it.

Thank you to the lovely
Estelle Gillingham who literally
turns 'dark' into 'light'.

My friends and family...
love you guys!

PREFACE

'you teach best, that which you most need to learn...'
Richard Bach

Why I wrote this book...

I wrote this book and created this system to remind myself and others to:

- Release your Money Blocks
- Reprogramme your Money Mindset
- Energise your goals and your business
- Create sustainable abundance

I wish someone had handed me a copy of this money making system when I was in my early 20's. My life would have been very different and I could have spent time doing things I love and getting paid to do so too!

I would have been able to do away with all the doubt and worry and uncertainty around making money.
I would have worked through my money blocks,

embraced good money habits and then moved straight into living my most abundant, wonderful version of life possible.

I started this preface with the words: 'you teach best what you most need to learn' ...this is really significant saying for me, it has a special energy about it and throughout my life it has popped up, reminding me to reflect on what I most need to learn to do.

I taught myself first and now I am teaching it to others. And aslo enjoying the journey of learning alongside others as they improve their money mindsets and create their sustainable wealth and abundance. That's right, althought I have come such a long way, I will be learning alongside others as they take their first tentative steps toward achieving their wealth and abundance goals. I hope I never stop learning, but more than that, I recognise that the best way to improve your wealth is by practicing the techniques and strategies outlined in this book.

Think of it like a 'practice'. The 'practice' of making money and turning your fortune around. It is a continuous circle of clearing, healing, forgiving and earning. Once you have cleared one money block and reached a new goal, your next money block and goal will show up. I continue to grow and learn alongside the lovely sensitive souls who have shared their 'money blocks' and 'magical abundant wins' on our private message boards and group pages.

This system is designed to support you as your

circumstances change. Growing in stages and building on the foundation of the first goal and achievements means that it is easier to achieve the second goal etc. The system helps keep you motivated and your vibration high as you walk the path to your own personal wealth and abundance.

I am also sure, that as sensitive souls, you can 'feel' how uncertain the world feels right now. Everything is changing at high speed. The rules of 'how to live' and 'how to make money' have changed exponentially and you may feel uncomfortable, challenged and shaken. That is why harnessing your intuition and looking inward, using your unique gifts and drawing on mother nature and the solid energy of Mother Earth to create abundance will help you feel grounded, strong, confident.

I also believe that time is precious. We all have the same amount of time afforded to us and what we do with it is so important. I have, therefore, outlined who this book is for and who it is NOT for.

WHO THIS BOOK IS FOR.

This money insight system is for anyone who:
- Doesn't gel well with traditional 'hard hitting' sales techniques.
- Runs their own business and wants to improve it.
- Wants to grow their business.
- Wants to start their own business.
- Has an idea of what they want to make/sell.
- Wants to break out of their 9-5 life of working

for someone else.
- Wants to build on an already successful business.
- Would like to fine tune their financial goals.
- Would like to improve their abundance.
- Would like to create a sustainable flow of money.
- Needs motivation and inspiration to take their product/service to the next level.
- Needs motivation and inspiration to keep their attention on their goals.
- Finds it difficult to get new customers.
- Who likes animals and mother nature.
- Who understands there are physical and metaphysical ways to improve wealth.
- Enjoys and feels the benefit of guided meditation from time to time.

This book is NOT for anyone who:

- Makes money easily
- Is a natural born sales person
- Has absolutely no idea what they want to do or make or sell in order to make money.

If you have no idea as to what you want to do right now... and I mean 'literally no idea', if you feel that you are so blocked with resistance and cannot begin to think of where to start then it would be my great honour to introduce you to the lovely Estelle Gillingham who runs the 'Activate Your Magic' course.

Estelle will take you through the journey of

discovering who you came here to be.

Estelle will help you:
Crack the code on doing what you love and bring your unique healing abilities into the world by being true to your highest nature…
…rather than listening to everyone else (including your own self doubt!)

www.estellegillingham.com/
activate-your-magic-group-programme/

GETTING STARTED

0 -1000 in 10 seconds:

If you are as impatient as I am then you will want to get started right away.

You can always come back and read the rest of the introduction and the 'Money Insights' at another time.

I am impatient to get the show on the road too, and once I have evidence that the system is working, then I like to invest my time in finding out more. I therefore understand where you are coming from and have simplified the starting process.

This is your life, your financial journey and I believe you should structure it in a way that suits you. So either read the whole book from start to finish, or skip the first 11 chapters and crack on with 'making money'. You can come back to them when you see the evidence of how well they work.

I wish you a magical, life changing journey!

STEP ONE:
Shuffle your cards and pull 3 in random order from the
pack. Place the 3 cards in the card holder provided.

STEP TWO:
Have a quick read through the meaning and lesson
for each of the cards from their corresponding chapter
in this book. Take on board any changes you need
to make to your daily routine in order to change your
fortune for the better.

STEP THREE:
Over the next week, look out for synergies in your
everyday work life with the 3 cards you have pulled.

Opportunities will come up and you will start to develop
the new habits that you need in order to help you
achieve your wealth and abundance.

Refer back to the cards often and re-read any chapters
to help cement the ideas in your mind and anchor the
positive lessons into your daily life and routines.

STEP FOUR:
At the end of the week, return these 3 cards to the deck,
shuffle well and choose another 3 cards to help you
focus on achieving your money goals over the following
week, and so on.

Choose a different set of 3 cards every week.

STEP FIVE:
When you have time, go back and read the book in more detail. Log on to the website and activate your free bonuses. Sign up to the brag page: www. abundance-magic.co.uk/peackock.
And start living your ABUNDANT MAGICAL LIFE.

STEP SIX:
If you keep getting the same or similar cards with similar messages you may be overlooking something very obvious. A block or resistance to money that has been with you for so long that you cannot even see it anymore.

There are lots of tips and helpful hints throughout the book to guide you on your journey. Also, visit the bonus section on our website for help on getting deeper insights into your money blocks and self-sabotaging behaviour.

www.abundance-magick.co.uk/BONUS

I'm so pleased you have started your *Abundant Magic Money Making Journey.*

If you join our online group, you will find it a safe haven, a place where you can share your hopes, dreams, triumphs and epic fails!

I cannot wait for you to get started.

GOOD LUCK!

CHAPTER ONE - INSTINCTS

'When the student is ready the teacher appears...'
Buddha

Are you ready to live your best life?

Have you read every book about money and still cannot get any traction on your goals or money in the bank?

I had, I was addicted to doing anything that would help me receive more money.

I felt wealthy in my dreams and yet I would wake every day to the harsh reality that my bank balance was scarily low... I even spent a few years in overdraft and I had bad credit card debt. (Yes, me really)

Every bill through the post was a painful reminder that I was in trouble. It wasn't just that particular bill that was the problem, it was the fact that I had no idea how to get out of the huge ever-widening 'lack of money' pit I was living in. It was like living in a big, bad bear trap... the bills were coming in fast and furiously and I had no way of settling them. It seamed like there was no way to get out of the hole. I just couldn't get a foothold or grip on my finances. I was trying to climb out but I just kept slipping back into the hole. There were times when I wasn't sure where I would live and how I would pay rent at the end of the month.

I remember one month I had to borrow money to buy food. That was mortifying...

I didn't know how to change my situation and it seemed to be getting worse.

I even got into the very bad habit of not opening mail, it was too scary. Every time I opened another bill my energy and emotions would plummet.

I didn't just have a lump in my throat, it was in my chest and stomach too. I was living in a state of fear and anxiety, the kind that feels like it has no edge to it. Normally a problem has a beginning, a middle and an end. Thereby making it easier to tackle, easier to break down into manageable bits to deal with. For me, this problem had no end in sight. It affected and infected every part of my life. I felt overwhelmed and suffocated... I couldn't think straight.

I could never seem to shake off the feeling of dread, no matter how well I slept, the feeling of despair would fill me up and drag my energy straight down again, within a few moments of waking I would be spiralling in worry and fear all over again.

The problem was compounding too. One thing after another... it felt like the world was kicking me whilst I was down. It just seemed like the universe was delivering bad news after bad news after bad... a never-ending cycle.

The other thing I will never forget is how it affected my confidence. I realised the quickest way to take away my confidence was to take away my money... just remove any hope of paying my bills every month.

It was the feeling of lack of 'self-sufficiency' that I struggled with most.

Feelings of overwhelm and alarm ran through me every moment of every day and in every cell of my body. I felt alone, abandoned, desperate, shaken, unhappy and hopeless.

Every time I saw my bank balance I had a sinking feeling... I felt like I was never going to get out of this cycle... all my dreams of being wealthy felt impossible to achieve.

I also held a lot of self-blame, guilt and embarrassment around this problem. The reality was that I was running my own graphic design and branding business and I felt embarrassed that I hadn't made it a huge financial success.

Wow... that is no way to live. It was awful!!!

The strangest thing was that despite these circumstances, I was sure I was meant to be wealthy.

I had this tiny little glimmer of hope that could sometimes be felt. When I wasn't completely exhausted from worrying about money and when the occasional good bit of news found its way to me, the cloud would part just enough so that I could see a spark of something that I wanted to hold on to and find more of.

I hadn't always been in this financial hole. I had previously had a good career, great salary and prospects... so why was this happening. 'I should know better' I thought to myself... 'where am I going wrong?'

I know now that I was not listening to my instincts.

I know I was not following the path I was meant to follow. Somehow, along the way, I had lost myself. I had ignored my instincts, allowed other people to make me small, I had listened to their ideas about who I am and who I should be. I had given them my power... and I was definitely not respecting myself and my goals, my hopes and dreams were nowhere to be found in my daily life.

It felt like I was sleepwalking through life, putting one foot in front of the other and just focusing on getting through the next few minutes - that was all I could cope with.

I couldn't think about a whole day or week or month or year. Just this next hour...'how to survive the next hour!'

One of the reasons I let this go on for so long is because I was embarrassed about the fact that this had happened to me in the first place. I had allowed this to happen or I had attracted it into my life and it was deeply troubling to admit it and own it.

I also secretly hoped that the circumstances would change without me doing anything about it.

I never thought of myself as a such a failure before, and now I was staring down the barrel of self-imposed disaster... me, of all people!

There was a defining moment when I was snapped out of things and this was during a visit with my Granddad.

He lived alone, as my grandmother had passed over a decade ago. I was chatting to him about something and he, for some reason started asking me about my personal life. This is not something he normally did, we normally chatted about the weather and we had long conversations reminiscing about the past.

I opened up about a few problems, which was also unusual for me, as I had decided not to burden any of my family members with what I was going through.

I explained what was happening in my personal life in terms of being unhappy in a marriage that wasn't working. He sat bolt upright in his chair and in rather animatedly exclaimed ... ' what!!!... no one does that to my granddaughter!!!'

13

I felt the shock of energy run through me... this is the reaction I should be having to what was happening to me and I should be running in the opposite direction.

He was so right... I wasn't raised this way, I wasn't raised to give my power away, I was raised to stand strong and own my own destiny. Why was I even putting up with this in the first place?

I had become so meek and mild, and so mousy that I had lost my way completely. I wasn't being true to myself or my 'higher self' or living the life I was meant to live. All the problems in my personal life were leaking into my business and the business was becoming weak and meek and mild too.

I made a decisions right then and there that I had to turn things around. As part of my journey to wealth and abundance, I started listening to my instincts and working my way back to the life I knew I was destined to live.

There wasn't one specific thing that turned things around for me. It was a multitude of elements that worked together in order to get me from where I was... 'living in a black hole'... to where I am now and ultimately these will get me to where I am going in the future.

This list includes the main elements:
1. INSTINCTS - trust them, they are there for a reason.
2. SELF-RESPECT - if you don't respect yourself,

no one else will and that includes money.

3. FORGIVENESS - forgiving yourself and others is critical to reaching your goals.
4. SELF-SABOTAGING - behaviour and finding a pattern interrupter to prevent it from recurring.
5. ACKNOWLEDGE - positive experiences.
6. SYMBOLS create some for your subconscious mind to relate to and focus on.
7. DE CLUTTERING - everything
8. VISUALISATION and meditation techniques to keep your vibration high.
9. ALTERNATIVES - think about alternatives to current behaviour in order to move forward. Example: Creating good money habits
10. RESPONSIBILITY - take responsibility for your own life, money and destiny.
11. TRUTH - being true and facing fears head on instead of hiding behind something or someone.

(These 11 lessons are spread out across all the animal cards and each is explained in its own chapter at the beginning of this book.)

I started small... first and foremost I started to listen to my instincts. I allowed just a bit of respect for myself to creep in here and there.

This wasn't easy at first. It meant that I had to face the reality that a lot of things in my life had to change... and I had to make a lot of big changes that were very scary and uncomfortable. I had to change where I lived, most of my friends and even get divorced... shock horror!

Change can be difficult in the best of circumstances but when you are at your lowest ebb in life, they seem impossible. However, once you have made the decision to trust your instincts and trust that you need to do what it takes to get out of your 'bear trap', things start to move and improve exponentially.

You also need to trust the concept that 'you can do what you set out to do, you do have what it takes to make your life the best life possible'.

I am delighted to report that every day that I stuck to my guns and trusted my instincts, I felt ONE THOUSAND times better than I did the day before. You can give me those odds any day of the week!

Spurred on by my success, I kept at it, following the list previously mentioned and tackling each bit repeatedly.

I found that I had to spend quite a bit of time meditating on each element. Asking myself, right, what to do next?

In order to circumvent the time consuming task of working out what to do next, I came up with the animal card system.

It has broken all these subjects into bite-size pieces and by choosing 3 new cards every week, you can focus on just the bits you need to focus on that week.

This takes the guesswork out of knowing what to do next.

Your subconscious will help you choose the cards that you need to work on that day/week/month.

I'm sure none of you reading this book right now have to go through the drastic changes I went through to start your abundance journey.

However, I hope it's helpful for you to know that if this system can help someone like myself, 'climb out of a big-ass bear trap', then it could certainly help others who are wanting to make some improvements to their abundance.

No matter where you are in your abundance journey the 'money insights' system can help you to make positive improvements and get you closer to living your most abundant, magical life.

FAST FORWARD A FEW YEARS ON

I had turned the business around, improved the type of clients I worked with, created a better sustainable business model, improved my finances, paid off all my debt.

I manifested £50,000 into my bank account. Met and married the right 'Mr Right'. We have an abundant life in more ways than just financial.

Abundance comes in many forms and I would like to refer to it as 'charmed'. I feel like we live a 'charmed life'. We have fabulous friends and neighbours, we live in the best village in the best country in the world.

HOWEVER, I STILL KNEW SOMETHING WAS MISSING.

Yes, I could pay all my bills every month and we were paying off the mortgages of two properties, we had a good life together but there was no BIG financial buffer that I desperately craved and I was working fairly hard, 'long hours' and I felt like I needed to do something BIG to create this change.

The money insights were still working and still are working, our branding business is going from strength to strength. I say our, because hubby has joined now... 'hooray', another goal on the wish list ticked off!

But the money insights needed to be applied to something else. I wanted to create a passive income to run alongside the everyday business.

I knew that I needed to create financial security and financial resources that would pay dividends every month.

I decided to write a book, something I had been thinking of doing for many years. Over the years, I had started to write books and then couldn't finish them, I didn't feel inspired.

I kept writing about the branding business, which I love but I felt like it had 'all been done before'.

Does the world really need another book on logo

design? Perhaps... and maybe once I'm ready, that book will take shape and be born... watch this space!

I kept trying to find my inspiration and I finally turned a corner by thinking about what inspires me most in my every day experience. What makes me get out of bed early in the morning and rush into the day?

When I did that exercise, it all became crystal clear:

Putting into writing all the steps, 'physical steps' and 'metaphysical steps' I use to create wealth and abundance in my own life I can now share it with others.

This book outlines the system I use to increase my financial abundance and will give you some practical advice and tools to get you there too.

There are also some 'life-changing' meditations that you can practice to speed up the process and get you on track faster.

It will still be your responsibility to get there. However, having been on this journey myself, I'm so pleased to say these things do work and I am confident that if you put in the work and get your mind focused on 'money mindsets', you will get there.

The book is set up so that you can choose to do the

PHYSICAL exercises

and/or

METAPHYSICAL exercises.

The system is also designed to keep you motivated and engaged in getting the financial abundance you know you deserve.

WHY PHYSICAL AND METAPHYSICAL

I have always felt like I understand both physical and metaphysical worlds simultaneously and can often be an interpreter between the two worlds.

For example, some of my clients in our branding business are 'bohemian, yogi, artist' types who live in a super-spiritual world and spend about 91 per cent of their time 'up there' or 'in the zone'...they would prefer to be there 100% of their time but their human needs bring them back down to earth to do the necessary from time to time.

When we are designing marketing materials for them and their fabulous 'out of this world' businesses, I often explain to them that the western world needs concrete facts to help them to understand this product or service.

In order to sell products or services, we have to talk about the benefits and what pain it solves... the 'yogi' types are often mystified by this idea. But we get there in the end!

At the same time, if a person who spends 91% of their time in concrete facts needs to understand the metaphysical aspects of the world... I can often break it down for them into bite-size easy to understand bits.

They might not 'get it' completely but at least they understand why it exists.

And more and more factual people are realising that they cannot deny the benefits of their experience of the 'yogi' services or products, even if they don't understand them completely.

My point is that I understand both worlds. I feel the benefit of doing both sets of exercises and because my money goals are so high, I have such a lot of work to do to achieve them that I feel I need to throw 'everything at it'!

I also wanted to respect both types of people and give them the option to choose which tools they will use to achieve their goals.

We are all so different and I love that about us humans ...we all experience things in different ways. The truth is, a '91% factual person' is unlikely to be reading this book, it will seem far to 'woo woo' and ungrounded in reality for them.

I'm sure some of you will appreciate both options and can enjoy the journey of finding out which works best for you. The important thing is that you have purchased this book and you are now on your way to your most magical abundant life. Well done for taking the first step!

CHAPTER TWO - SELF RESPECT

"Our self respect tracks our choices. Every time we act in harmony with our authentic self and our heart, we earn our respect. It is simple, every choice matters"
Dan Coppersmith

Do you love and respect yourself?
Show yourself that you do, every day... all the time! The universe will reward you for it.

I talk a lot about your subconscious / the universe throughout this book and the positive things it looks for on a daily basis. It is designed to help you and depending on what you show it will depend on what it continues to give you.

But this chapter is all about what your subconscious observes you REJECTING.

It may sound weird at first but it is important that you

become very discerning about who and what you allow into your life. Including the types of clients, you deal with.

Some people might start to call you fussy or picky... and you should turn to them and say ... 'HELL YEAH'!!! I'm a regular 'fuss pot'! I'm picky, I'm fussy, discerning, choosy, conscientious, discriminating, finicky, scrupulous, careful, conscionable, exacting, fastidious, finical, hard to please, nit-picking, pernickety, picky, picky, picky...

If your subconscious notices that you will bend your rules when it comes to most money circumstances it won't take you seriously. It will be quite happy to deliver poor quality customers time and again. It's attitude will be 'if you can't be bothered, then neither can I'

This is a particularly tough subject when you are just starting out and you believe you need to take on any work, any client, anywhere, any time.

This may be true for a while, but if you practice all the other techniques in this book then you will start to attract the right clients and this should no longer be a problem.

There are many reasons why you might be willing to bend your rules or put your goals on hold for a while. Or even put the needs of some clients ahead of your own - by this I mean take on clients who really can't afford you, but you know you can help them and you do it anyway.

The reason I did it, was because I was used to doing it. Being the oldest of 4 children, I learned at an early age that my needs were not the most important, it was important to put the youngest person's needs first, share everything and put yourself last. These are all very admirable qualities in the context of family and they have ensured the survival of the human species and I don't think we could live as humans without them, however, I made the mistake of transferring all these ideas into my business.

Before I knew it, I was helping everyone for very little money. Working long hours and not having enough money to pay my bills at the end of the month.

I believe you can still be a great, well respected person, get on well with your clients, be generous with your time and deliver a 5-star service, provided it works both ways!

If you don't respect yourself and your money goals, your clients won't and your ever-watchful subconscious mind won't either.

An example:

I have a client, lets call him 'Sam'.

Sam wanted me to make his business the centre of my attention all day every day (all night too if possible).

He also wanted to pay me less than the going rate for the work I did for him.

I admired Sam's passion for his business, I appreciated his energy and drive, I also started to work with him knowing the fact that I was being underpaid but hoping that the circumstances would change, that he would see how hard I worked for him and would appreciate me and pay me more money.

Of course, you can imagine, he did not appreciate my services in that way, he did not pay me more money.

A few months after we started to work together my business grew and we got quite busy. I condensed his work into fewer hours and he was still getting more than he should have for what he was paying me.

He did not like this idea at all.

He was also in a position where he had built up his business to have quite a few staff doing the work for him so he had plenty of time to hound me with phone calls and emails all day and night.

Being the conscientious person I am, I decided to continue working with him and stretched my workdays into longer and longer hours.

Every time I invoiced Sam he would spend a significant amount of time talking me into lowering my prices... and although I would argue each time about how much time each project took, eventually I would give in and reduce my prices!!! ... crazy right?

Something had to give...

I explained to Sam that the my fees on certain elements were non negotiable and that I charge less than the going rate for his work, and therefore I should be paid the fee on the invoice. He basically ignored these new boundaries that I set up.

Eventually, I started to hold back more and more. I would take longer to deliver the work because I had other clients that were paying full price and obviously they had to take priority, it's only fair, would you agree?

I was exercising all the other fundamentals described in this book and the work was pouring in.

Sam eventually got so frustrated with me not putting his business at the centre of my world that he decided to go elsewhere. He tried many other brand and graphic design agencies in the area.

The first time this happened, I felt a prickle of annoyance flow through my whole body, you know the type that makes your face feel prickly with some sort of red hot angry feeling, it was just a natural reaction which I let go as fast as possible.

I also now know that I had started on the wrong foot. Sam had learned that I would bend my own rules if he asked me to. I needed to take responsibility for this. It was my own fault that I was not getting paid what I was worth.

On one hand it's always difficult when you lose a client but on the other hand, if they won't pay you what you are worth… good riddance!!

Over the next few months I would, sometimes, late at night, receive an email or a 'What's App' message from Sam about a project that had gone horribly wrong, and could I possibly fix it?

Luckily I had done all the forgiveness work outlined in the next chapter so it was very easy to pick up where we left off… this time, however, I put my prices up, the invoices were paid without argument and Sam continues to be a great client. He even refers me to other people. Result!

The point I'm making with the example above is that at some point I found some self-respect, stuck to my guns and chose to be true to my business objectives. I set up boundaries, made the client aware of them and stuck to them.

I give great service, I'm always on time and budget, I communicate well to let clients know what status the project is at and if a client doesn't respect that then they don't deserve my services.

I know this is easier said than done… I lived it… it was difficult, but I promise you will be so glad when you create and stick to your business objectives.

It takes practice and evidence that 'everything will be OK' to feel confident with this subject. I would suggest as always, that you start small. Pull back a bit. Put your prices up a bit. Don't do anything drastic. But do take action. If you are terrified about losing clients and lose sleep over it then I suggest you read and start practising the other parts of this book first and once you have the hang of getting new clients in easily, then come back to this part and challenge yourself to raise your prices again.

If you are wired, like I am, to always give too much, always put other's needs first then you may have to re visit this chapter often. I will let you in on a secret here.

I have to re visit this chapter often!

Even though my business is a success, I do from time to time get tested, by the universe or my subconscious mind.

A project will crop up that is not quite right for my business and I have to be firm and stick to my guns about my prices... or let it go. I have a few other brand and graphic design agencies that I can pass work on to, if it isn't the right fit for me, then I can hand it to someone else who would love it.

Practicing self respect doesn't just affect your business, it works well in your personal life too. If you find you attract people into your life that walk all over you, you can use the techniques outlined here to prevent this behaviour.

Put up some personal boundaries as well as business ones and watch how your life changes... you may lose some friends along the way ...but are they actually true friends... are they friends with you for the right reasons?

If someone doesn't want the best for you, then consider the idea that they are not actually your friend!

The cards will help you know when it's time to re visit this subject.

CHAPTER THREE - FORGIVENESS

Once bitten, twice shy...

FORGIVENESS AND OVERCOMING MONEY BLOCKS

The money will follow the path of least resistance, but you have to actually remove the resistance, you'll reap huge rewards when you do.

The way to remove resistance is normally through forgiveness. For most people, this is a really big, messy business. The reason why this is such a tricky area is that forgiveness normally involves other people.

Forgiving yourself should be easier. If you don't already, get into the habit of forgiving yourself, tell yourself you have learned from the mistake and move on.

Once bitten, twice shy...
If someone has done you a bad turn, if you forgive them, are you opening up the gateway to them hurting you

again? And why should they feel relief, after all, their actions were so awful and painful, they really hurt you!

Should they be allowed to get away with it?

At the root of this problem, however, is the idea that the person who is truly being hurt by the lack of forgiveness is the victim. So if you don't forgive someone their slight against you, you are the one that stays bound to their action and the negativity around this action... forever!

If someone has done something to you that is fairly innocuous then by all means let them know that they are forgiven and you can both move on.

I personally do forgive and have forgiven lots of people their slights against me, and I even discuss it with them too. If I believe someone truly means that they are sorry, I find it very easy to forgive them and also let them know I have done so. However, if someone does something repeatedly and asks for forgiveness for the same thing over and over again then I would consider an alternative action.

If possible, remove yourself from their world completely and take steps to create a world for yourself where you are surrounded by very positive people who are on your side and mean you no harm.
When I have been wronged myself and experienced huge amounts of heartache caused by the actions of one specific person, who shows no signs of remorse and who continues to wreak havoc in my life, in ever increasing doses, I have often chosen to 'NOT' tell

them that they are forgiven.

The reason I have decided not to tell them is that I am afraid that if I do tell them, they may then decide that it was so easy to get forgiveness this time, that it will be easy to obtain forgiveness in the future and they will therefore continue their poor behaviour toward me and possibly others.

If I tell them I forgive them, I will then bear the brunt of their negative actions again and again and again. It would be like I'm enabling them to continue their poor treatment of myself and others.

Let's face it, some people are not ready to deal with forgiveness or ready to deal with change.

The best thing I have found is to forgive them energetically and feel the release and benefit of this for myself. Is it selfish?... yes.. it is selfish... but what is the alternative?

Should I spend hours engaged in conversation with them, whilst they work out their emotional drama?

Do I want to spend one more second of my precious time dealing with someone else's demons?

I have still forgiven these people energetically. This is one of the most delicious and freeing feelings in the world. I also, at the same time forgave myself for allowing myself to be in the way of that behaviour in the first place.

I must suggest that you exercise common sense when dealing with your forgiveness of people. Only you can decide how to deal with the situation going forward. Only you can decide how to approach the subject of forgiveness with another person.

This is a personal choice. It's totally up to you.

I urge you to try it on something small first, so you get a feel for how it works and how liberating it is and then tackle the bigger forgiveness issues later.

Once you have forgiven someone for your heartache, you will be lifting your vibrational energy field and moving some resistance in your life.

This is especially true when it comes to your wealth and abundance goals. If you have experienced a bad business deal, or had a run in with a horrible business person/employee, you may have some money blocks around improving your business.

The way to test this is to write down a few things you could do to improve your business.

Example:
- Employ more staff
- Set up new systems and processes
- Purchase and use modern software to save time
- Get more business via marketing
- Improve sales through speaking engagements

If you then decide to take action on one of these tasks

but discover that you cannot move forward for some reason then you may have a 'big, old money block' around this subject.

Think of money blocks as a 'monkey on your back'

Here's an example of a 'money block' I had in terms of growing my business.

I had grown the branding business and I was working really hard at one point, I really needed some help.

I knew I needed to employ at least one freelancer to help with the work load.

Many years ago, I had managed a team of about 6 people and 3 freelancers, and although it was rewarding, I had found it was hard work. It felt like I spent all day managing the team instead of doing my own work. I would give them all work to do then settle down to do my own (lion share) of the work, only to be interrupted half an hour later with a query. Times this by 9 people and you can imagine. I couldn't get any work done. So I would end up working later and later to complete the work load.

I found it exhausting!

I often thought that if I got rid of all the staff, although I would need to work really long hours to complete the work load, at least it would all get done without thousands of exhausting interruptions. This is a very poor solution.

Instead, I set up boundaries and some rules. It was chaos at first but everyone eventually 'got the memo'.

I insisted that with every query the person came to me with, they would have to supply 3 possible answers. And they were only allowed to ask the same question 3 times. Instead of asking me the same thing over and over again.

And I literally counted the times that they asked me the same question. I kept a journal and wrote their name down, the question and the amount of times they asked this same question.

I would say: 'George, this is the second time that you are asking me the same question. You only have one more chance to ask me the same question.'

It raised some eyebrows within my team. They were so used to me solving all their problems and holding their hand through every little task that this was a bit uncomfortable for them.

It made them start to think before absent mindedly interrupting me with questions. It made them 'sit up' and notice that they need to take responsibility for themselves on a daily basis.

It also revolutionised my day. It cut the amount of interruptions down to about a quarter of previously asked questions and I was able to get on with my work.

FAST FORWARD A FEW YEARS AND NOW I RUN MY

OWN BUSINESS...

There came a time when I needed help and wanted to employ freelancers. I had to really push myself through this block. The memory of 'the pain of training people' to be great employees was still quite painful and irksome and prevented me from rushing out to seek help.

With a small amount of time spent thinking about my problem, I was able to identify what was holding me back and reason that: 'now that I am so much more experienced at setting boundaries and managing people' it will not be a problem to employ people to help me move some mountains.

I realised I would be able to set out the boundaries and clearly define roles and responsibilities up front.

I also had to forgive myself for feeling afraid of the work it will take to get freelancers 'up to speed' in my new business. I had to forgive my previous employees for being 'hard work'. I had to forgive myself for 'not setting up good boundaries' in the first place.
I was then able to get that monkey off my back! I have amazing freelancers that I work with on a daily basis.

Before I employed anyone, I set the intention that all the freelancers would be fabulous, like minded souls with integrity and a strong work ethic like mine.

This has allowed me to grow the business and improve my wealth and abundance.

Take a few moments now to list all the monkeys you have on your back.

TOP TIP:
Write down the date that you forgive the person or yourself and put a new date in your diary about 3 or 4 weeks after this date.

When you arrive at this new date in your diary, look back and notice if something significant has changed to your abundance stream. Look out for any positive progress. I am confident that you will notice a marked improvement.

Up to this point in this chapter we have focused on PHYSICALLY forgiving people and yourself.

I have also developed a METAPHYSICAL guided meditation to help you to move through your forgiveness journey faster.

Login to our members area and work through the meditation online:
www.abundance-magic.co.uk/FORGIVENESS

CHAPTER FOUR - SELF-SABOTAGE

'We sabotage the great things in our lives because deep down, we don't feel worthy of having these great things' Taressa Riazzi

Self-sabotage is normal, you may experience a blip when things start to move in the right direction.

There are three main situations when self-sabotage happens:

- Something amazing comes into your life but you make sure you destroy it
- You have the opportunity to do something positive for yourself or your business but instead you do nothing
- You know what you need to do to make money but you put it off and allow yourself to get distracted

I have two great examples...

Example One:

If you are like me, when you are focused on your work you go into a 'zone' I'm not sure what you want to call it, perhaps... 'channelling' or 'being in the zone'. This is where my best creativity happens, I can lose hours and hours at a time and I really enjoy being in this place.

However, when I first started my branding business, I had to do everything myself, including answering the phone. So I might be deep in thought 'in the zone', designing away, moving mountains and changing the landscape of a brand that I was working on and the phone rings, it's a client who would like a price for a specific project.

Being filled with 'money block's in those days, meant that I had a make-shift list of prices tucked away somewhere in the recess of my brain and I would try to draw on this memory to give a 'live quote' for the client who was on the other end of the phone.

Pricing was a subject that I did not enjoy at all in those days so the list of prices for my work was tucked far, far, far away, in a dark, dusty, forgotten box, in a cupboard, under some indescribable brain junk.

Invariably I would get flustered at this point, trying to retrieve this information and being quite uptight about the idea that 'client is king' ...and should therefore not be 'kept waiting'...in this flustered state, I would blurt out a price way below what I should have quoted.

41

So annoying!!! ...

Hours later I would have time to stew on the idea that
I had set myself up to fail. I was sabotaging myself
and my business by not quoting the correct amount
of money. Something great had happened: 'a client
phoned looking to commission me to do some work'...
and instead of being clear headed and quoting
responsibly, I just blurted out a figure way below what I
should be charging.

It took me a while to realise what I was doing. I
eventually decided that the best way for me personally
to deal with this particular problem was to ask the client
if I could send them the quote via email.

This really turned things around for me.

It gave me the extra few minutes or even half an hour I
needed to think through the new project carefully and
then charge appropriately.

I could have had a 'printed price list' on my desk to
refer to when the phone rang... that could also help. But
invariably the type of work I do is priced in accordance
with the complexity of the project so I cannot always
have a 'one size fits all' price list.

A few years later, I met a new supplier, who's work was
priced far too low.

I insisted on putting her price for the work up by £10 per
hour. She was really uncomfortable about this at first but

she soon got the hang of it.

In hindsight, I was actually quite lucky that she got the hang of it so quickly, because she obviously had money block issues and doing this could have created a problem between us. She could have freaked out, deciding not to work with me and I could have lost out on receiving the lovely gift of working with her.

As and when this subject comes up these days, I am very careful when discussing the prices with suppliers who need to raise their fees. I gently broach the subject and sometimes suggest they read this book and let them get comfortable in their own space and time rather than foisting a price increase on them.

Some people reading this book would question why I would want to raise prices that suppliers charge me. The answer is quite simple: If I enjoy working with a supplier and they have a great work ethic, they supply a great service, always delivering on time and budget then I would really like to continue working with them going forward. In order for them to have a sustainable business, they need to be priced accurately.

Example Two:

I had a real block around asking clients for money. It felt awkward, really strange, it felt like I was asking someone for something really inappropriate.

I felt embarrassed that I needed something. It felt like I was asking for help or a handout. As though for some weird reason I was being really needy and annoying.

Because of this, I would leave it until the last minute to invoice clients.

I was also under the misguided impression that once I sent an invoice, my client would automatically pay it (this was the way I paid my suppliers, after all). I certainly would never order something if I had no intention of paying for it. Or if I couldn't afford it.

The fact that some of them didn't pay me on time made me feel even worse about the subject. I felt embarrassed enough asking them for the money in the first place and then when they didn't pay me it seemed to strengthen the distorted idea in my head that I didn't deserve to be paid.

Fast forward a few years, I now know that some people genuinely don't see invoices as a top priority or miss them (not intentionally) but there are plenty who avoid them on purpose.

PHYSICAL SOLUTION

To break the self sabotaging behaviour I invented a system that I decided to stick to like super glue!

It took me a few practices (I don't mind admitting) but eventually I was like gorilla glue...stuck to my business systems and procedures.. and now I absolutely will not budge until:

A: I have received 50% of the project fee 'up front' clearly stating on the invoice that the balance is due on completion.

B: 100% payment up front

C: The client has signed a contract stating that they will pay for the services over 12 months in 12 equal payments to be taken on ... day of the month price clearly outlined. etc.

I have also written up these terms on my website and they go out with every quotation.

It's a personal choice how you run your business but this does come back to Chapter 2's discussion about self respect.

If you do not respect yourself, your business, your money or your goals, your clients won't either. If you don't believe me, give it a try:

When your next new client comes along put them onto a payment system that suits you straight away. Even if it feels awkward.

Once your subconscious mind sees your new client signing up and paying up front it will have all the evidence it needs to help you to achieve this new payment procedure going forward.

No more 'chasing money' for days on end. No more 'staying up late festering about late payments'... your money in your bank... result!

METAPHYSICAL SOLUTION

This self sabotage had a lot to do with emotional healing that I hadn't worked through.

I have created an energy healing that you can download from our website if you would like to fast track your self sabotage healing.

www.abundance-magic/sabotage

I also don't mind sharing at this point that self-sabotage can rear its ugly head time and again. Keep a watchful eye out for it and deal with it swiftly and efficiently.

CHAPTER 5 - ACKNOWLEDGE

ANCHORING IN POSITIVE EXPERIENCES

Your subconscious brain and conscious brain both agree on this point... if they can see EVIDENCE of positivity and improved results from their actions then they understand what to bring you 'more of'.

You may have spent years anchoring in bad experiences into your life. By this I mean you may have looked for evidence that you didn't deserve to be wealthy, that you weren't good enough to achieve greatness. You may have spent years telling yourself not to dream.

I know some parents believe that their 'lot in life' is really bad and that they are 'stuck with it' and in order to shield their children from the same disappointment that they go through, they actually teach their children to 'NOT hope' or 'NOT dream for too much'. If the child doesn't aim too high, then they won't come crashing down emotionally when they fail.

If you had a person in your life who taught you NOT to dream, and you are quite sure they were wrong, you can take steps to make positive changes and improve your destiny.

I personally want you to live a charmed life. One that is successful, happy and wealthy.

Most of my life I said out loud that I'm not lucky, and the universe went out of its way to make sure I was not lucky.

I eventually changed this to thinking that I was not lucky in winning prizes. But I knew I was lucky in other areas.

Unfortunately, I had done some fairly serious damage by beating this drum over and over again. I'm still very conscious of how much work I have to do on this subject. I have, I feel, moved mountains in clearing this block around money, but I do have a few more to move.

Many of us don't even realise how great our lives are and we take so much for granted.

Most animal chapters in this book deal with anchoring in positive experiences. I do go on about this a lot because of the amazing changes it has made in my business and my financial abundance.

The other reason is that a lot of self-help books and teachers talk about staying positive. But they don't teach you the little steps you can take to stay positive. By anchoring positive things into your everyday life you start your journey to being more positive, one 'high five' at a time...

How to stay positive and anchor in positivity:

ONE

'High five' anyone who will 'high five' you back on any positive achievement. Even if it's as small as finding a penny on the floor.

TWO

Keep a note of every single penny coming in and every single gift, even if its a 'free coffee'.

I have created a free App for you to download if you like using your phone for most things.

Alternatively, keep a fancy bound journal or an Micro Soft Word document where you can record every single 'WIN'.

The 'EVIDENCE' of anchoring positive experiences is very powerful and your subconscious mind becomes a bloodhound on the search for new positive experiences as soon as it knows it will get the reward of even a simple 'high five'.

THREE

I also suggest that you write a message that you send to yourself every evening via your phone or online calendar Or leave a note for yourself on your bedside table, mine says something like:

'I am so grateful for all that I have achieved today'.

This is an unusually powerful sentence. And the time of day is so important too.

I set the reminder to arrive on my watch and phone just before I'm getting into bed.

That way I end the day on a 'high'. I truly am grateful for all that I have done and because I feel so positive when I read the message every evening, my subconscious lingers on this positive feeling all night and when I awake the next morning I feel refreshed and ready to face the day, I am buzzing with excitement to get started.

My subconscious mind is so 'on board' and can't wait to get the next 'high five' and positivity anchored into my experience, it is like an excited puppy that knows no limitations.

I would say that I am '35% more productive' every day now, compared to before I had this affirmation reminder in my diary. I used to think I achieved quite a lot in a day and I was pleasantly surprised by how much more I now do each and every day.

You should beat your chest every time something positive happens, 'high five' your business partner/ spouse/friend/ dog or even me. I will respond as soon as I can.

www.abundance-magic.co.uk/peacock

It can take the universe a while to make the switch to a more positive place. So the sooner you start your positive talk and start acknowledging good things coming to you, the better.

Especially if you are a sensitive person, you may be allowing other people's thoughts in your head. But if you purchased this book and cards, your subconscious mind is telling you that you are ready to make the change and start acknowledging all the good things you have in your life.

This is particularly difficult when you feel like you are living in a 'bear trap' and the world around you is not anywhere you want it to be. If the problem seems insurmountable and so much needs to change that you feel overwhelmed, take heart, because we will do it together. I'm learning right along with you and shrinking the walls of my 'bear trap' every day.

It's best to take small steps. Read the chapter entitled 'WORMS' if this is a particularly big problem for you.

FIVE

Acknowledging that you are working on your money blocks and making big changes to your abundance is a great way to demonstrate to your subconscious mind that you are serious about making money. You may have spent years doing the reverse and now it will take time to undo the damage. But every step forward is a step in the right direction and things start to improve exponentially.

THE AXIS PRACTICE.

Align with your true axis and stay connected to your personal source energy. You can then channel your higher nature and be connected to the 'real you', the you that you were meant to be when you came to this planet. The 'you' that you intended to be before you even got here.

Trust me it was difficult for me to do this when I started. But it has been worth it. I was so out of alignment with who I truly am and I was so out of alignment with source energy. It is no wonder that I was living in the worst 'bear trap' hole in the ground imaginable.

But I can promise you that if you do these exercises and trust yourself that you can get back to 'you', 'your true self' it will be worth it... you are worth it.

Have you experienced the joy of finding parking in the shade on a sunny day, right outside the venue you were going to?

You arrived 10 minutes early, the parking was free, your host greets you with a nice cool drink and is genuinely pleased to see you.

Your business meeting goes well, you are the star of the show, the client signs the contract and you win the business... get the picture?

This is the type of day you have when you are aligned with your true axis and your personal source energy axis.

If you are in alignment with source and your higher self your true abundant nature will start to show through and your life could look like this.

The only catch is, you have to do this exercise every morning, like brushing your teeth, and sometimes, if something throws you off your axis during the day then it's worth repeating the exercise again and as soon as possible.

Scientists are trying to prove metaphysical phenomenon and are using systems and techniques to do so.

I find their talks very interesting but I don't spend much time on them. I don't need to because I have experienced first-hand, the amazing connection with the crystals at the centre of the wonderful planet we live on.

It seems to me that most animals have an automatic connection with these crystals too. It's only us humans that can become out of alignment with them and therefore out of tune with our own self and separated from our own 'higher self' axis.

In order to stay connected to our axis and reap the benefits of being aligned with mother earth and all the animals living on the planet, we can do something that I call the 'AXIS PRACTICE'.

Simply put, its about meditating or simply breathing in the energy from the centre of the earth into our chakras and also breathing in the energy of our higher self.

I like to do this exercise before I do anything else before I start my day.

ONE:

Take in a nice long deep breath to the count of 10 as you imagine the energy from the centre of the earth filling each of your chakras, one by one. Then hold for the count of 10 and release for a count of 10.

This exercise should be repeated 3 times

Do the same thing now whilst imagining breathing energy from the sky into your chakras for the count of 10... hold for 10 counts and then release for 10 counts.

Do this exercise 3 times.

I also like to imagine that the energy from the centre of the earth is like a nice long thick white beam of high vibrational energy that expands when it enters each chakra, filling up that section of my body with beautiful white light before it continues up to the next chakra and so on. The energy should also leave your crown chakra and continue up to your soul star chakra.

I have a habit of making a knot in the 'beam of light' at this point and securing it to my soul star chakra which sits about a half a meter above my crown chakra.

Every night when I go to sleep the knot seems to untie itself freeing the connection to source energy which then would appear to go off and help my subconscious with dreaming and dissecting the day's events, as well as preparing for the following day's activities.

This is why I have to do the 'AXIS PRACTICE' every day. In my experience source energy resets itself every night whilst I'm asleep.

I do the same thing with my 'higher self' energy, I fill up all my chakras and my body with high vibrational light and then I secure it to the earth star chakra that sits about a meter below my root chakra.

When I do this exercise I am given a vision of my best self. The person who I wish I could be every waking moment.

The vision I am shown is very similar to the 'fool' character from the Rider-Waite Tarot cards. Think of the posture of the fool, but with impossibly long, golden, blond hair and my clothes are made from gold spun silk. Its quite a beautiful vision and I look forward to seeing it each day.

I am sure everyone reading this book will have a completely different vision of their 'higher nature' character. If you feel like sharing then do send us a message on the www.abundance-magic.co.uk/peacock

I said at the start of this exercise that it took me a long time to do this exercise well.

Most of the members of my family including myself all seem to breathe with only the top part of our lungs.

We generally don't breath deeply, we don't fill our lungs and move our diaphragm with each breath... and this was a problem for me when I had to hold my breath for just 10 counts.

I found it very uncomfortable at first. I am pleased to announce that it only took a week to get it right and only took 2 weeks before amazing things started to happen.

My days improve exponentially when I do this exercise, positive, incredible, life-changing events occur when I do this exercise.

But don't take my word for it. try it now!

CHAPTER 6 SYMBOLS

THE POWER OF SYMBOLS

As I mentioned previously, I am not a psychologist and I don't have a degree in psychology or behavioural patterns, however, I have spent quite a lot of my time trying different ways to make money and testing various theories.

One theory has stood out from all others that I have tried and tested ...the theory that the subconscious mind prefers symbols to relate to and understand, rather than words.

Each person has a different interpretation of symbols and their meanings.

Example:

The first animal in this book is the 'Rat' and I talk a bit about this subject, for example, the Chinese revere the rat and yet, in our western cultures the rat can be associated with negativity and vermin. We each have a different view.

Throughout this book, I will encourage you to look past the traditional associations with the animals and instead consider their skills and positive attributes when you use this system.

But if you really dislike one of the animals I have used then by all means find your own animal to associate with in terms of overcoming your money blocks.

When we surround ourselves with symbols that make us feel happy and energised, it raises our vibration and helps us to focus on achieving our goals.

Just like the concept of surrounding yourself with positive people then your life improves and takes on a more positive direction.

Making upgrades in your life can have the same effect. If you make small upgrades to things, your subconscious mind notices these little upgrades and starts to find ways of bringing more of this experience into your life.

Example:

I was sharing an office which was 'okay', but it had lots of problems. One of the directors in one of the other companies I shared with had this idea that because I was there all day, and I did some work for their company, that I should therefore spend all day working on improving their business and their graphic design projects.

I found, after a while that going into the office was draining my energy. It was not a place where I could go to focus on achieving my own goals.

The way I managed to get out of this situation was by taking a few small steps toward bigger goals.

STEP ONE

I put together a dream board, with pictures and a story about the type of office environment I would like to work in. It's important to put both the picture and the story on the dream board. And if you create some big goals and then some little ones that can lead you up to the big goals you are far more likely to achieve the bigger goals.

One of the best ways to include the words for the story about your new office is to write down your ideal day. So you wake up in the morning ... and then what? Write down as much detail as possible.

Write down things like, I woke up in my gorgeous bed with 300 count Egyptian cotton sheets and looked out the window at my breathtaking view of.

I jumped out of bed eager to start the day with a fabulous cup of freshly brewed coffee. I sat drinking coffee and looking at the view of... whilst I planned my day...

I then... drove to the office which was only.... minutes away

I then ... made some sales calls
I then... designed a website
I then... ordered ingredients to cook in our restaurant
I then... walked over to the state of the art barn and milked our beautiful new dairy cows.
I then... baked 300 cookies for sale at the farmers market this weekend...
I then... invented a new flavour of chocolate for our vegan chocolate business....

You get the picture...

Include everything:

After lunch I ... met with the CEO of '...' to discuss how they want to distribute our products

After lunch I ... fed the horses and mucked out the stables

After lunch I ... held a refresher yoga class for local yoga teachers.

After lunch we ... met with the CEO '...' to discuss our new programme we developed

After lunch I... planned my speech for the conference coming up this weekend.

Include evening plans if you wish.

STEP TWO

What I started to do was make small symbols that represented the tasks I was going to do to get out of that office and into a better office. I chose symbols so that no one else around me would figure out what they meant. For example I had a little note tree on my desk that I could attach magnets to. Each magnet had a different symbol that represented an element of my dream board.

One magnet had a small image of an eagle on it and it reminded me to keep a sharp eye out for new opportunities. When I saw the symbol, it would remind me to phone or email existing customers and ask them if they were happy with the leaflet/website/ logo I had created for them and if they needed any more work.

One magnet was plane bright pink and I associated this with a giant pink balloon that was going to lift me up to reach my higher goals.

I had one magnet for de-cluttering and one to remind me not to self sabotage etc.

I can be an intensely private person and the last thing I wanted was other people seeing my exact goals and dreams on my desk and yet I recognised that I needed to have them around me in order to constantly remind myself to stay focused upon achieving my goals.

All to often in the past I had written up a dream board and then hidden it away from everyone including myself.

It's really difficult to manifest your goals when they are out of sight.

If I had the animal cards at that time I would have easily been able to put them on my desk in their neat holder and refer to them often throughout the week.

They would have been a lot easier to explain to fellow work colleagues. And I really appreciate their variety. I would sometimes become a bit 'blind' to my magnets on my desk. I got so used to seeing the same ones over and over again. It was a great day when I upgraded to the card system that come with this book.

Whenever I walked back to my office and desk, I would immediately notice the symbols and be reminded of my goals. It made me feel happy, energised and motivated.

With my renewed enthusiasm and feeling the energy of the animals on the magnets as my companions on my quest to improve, I was able to look past the idea of always sharing an office and get my conscious and subconscious mind focusing on a brighter future.

STEP THREE

Make a point of keeping your original dream boards, dream story and photo symbols and look back a few years later to tick off all the elements that you have actualised into your experience.

I am so pleased to say that every single one of those goals written on that magnetic note tree came true for me. I can tick them all off!

The other amazing thing about doing this is that my subconscious mind 'witnessed' me ticking off all these elements and it now has 'EVIDENCE' that this works and that even if it cannot see the end result now, my new dream board is working hard to deliver my new goals and ultimately, financial abundance.

METAPHYSICAL help to achieve your goals.

If you are as impatient as I am, then you can use this extra step to hurry things along.

By energising your goals, you are able to put more focus on them and bring them into your life faster.

Visit www.abundance-magic.co.uk/goals

FENG SHUI SYMBOLISM

The other very useful tool that I use is the art of Feng Shui. It is such a big subject and there are so many books about it, but the bit that I focus on and find useful is the money symbolism. I have also narrowed it down to a few key elements.

I do like symbols that have a purpose too. One of my

favourite objects in my office is a water fountain. It is quite small but it is a powerful symbol for me.

I have placed it in my money corner and I won't start work without first turning it on. It has become a bit of a ritual that I like to incorporate into my day.

The gentle sound of water in the background is very calming, the flow of the water in its cycle is significant in that it has a lovely never-ending rejuvenating quality and reminds me that my cup is overflowing with ideas, money and abundance of all things. Not just financial. I have a rich and abundant life.

The fountain has another more practical use too, it makes a slightly different sound when the water level gets a bit low, as soon as I hear this sound I fill it up again to ensure it is always working well.

This is a very practical reminder that all the plants in the room need watering too.

Before I started my journey to abundance back in the days when my whole world was falling apart, the last thing I would have done would be to take the time to have a water feature and plants around me, I would have considered this an absolute waste of my time to look after these objects. I now am so pleased to have them. I look at the plants that are so healthy and doing well and they remind me of how well I am doing on my abundant journey.

I have updated many elements in my life along this

abundant wealth journey. Each refreshing update is part of the bigger picture and the overall improved abundant journey.

One of the key elements of this book is sustainable growth and abundance. The best way to achieve this is through taking a lot of small steps to get to the big goals.

If you can, have a 'makeover', 'update' or 'refresh' anything in your life that is looking a bit tired or a bit out of date.

Remember small things make a BIG IMPACT on your subconscious mind so it won't cost a lot to start the process, but do make a start!

If you have old dying flowers or plants in your office, your subconscious is taking note, getting rid of dead and decaying things lifts your vibration and helps you feel elevated.

It might be a journal on your desk that is looking 'dog eared' and needs replacing or it may be your desk looks a bit like a 'pig sty'. If you take a few moments every day to spend updating things around you, these little updates are like magical little symbols that reinforce to your subconscious mind that you are serious about yourself and your money goals.

It will then take you seriously and action to support your goals and dreams.

CHAPTER 7 DE-CLUTTERING

THE POWER OF DE-CLUTTERING

Have you ever walked into someone else's office or business and felt the stuck energy of too much clutter?

And conversely have you walked into an office, restaurant or hotel and felt the wonderful crystal clear energy of a place that is well run and well looked after?

I'm sure this is not news to you, but when last did you de-clutter?
And I'm not just talking about your desk, though that is a good place to start!

I'm talking about your website, your goals, your marketing. When last did you refresh your logo?

AND FORGIVENESS

I also see forgiveness as a type of de-cluttering. If you have had a bad business experience you need to forgive all parties involved in order to move onward and upward.

We all forget from time to time to do the necessary de-cluttering that we need in order to progress.

If you've ever cleaned out a desk drawer and felt an incredible surge of satisfaction, you've experienced some of the magical and practical benefits of clearing clutter.

My personal definition of clutter is:

Anything that is not beautiful or useful.

And to borrow from Marie Kondo. You should only have items in your life that 'spark joy'

I humbly submit that we should apply this to people too. You should only work with people who 'spark joy' in your experience.

In Feng Shui philosophy, free-flowing energy creates health, wealth, love, and overall abundance.

Any clutter you have which could be physical things or emotional baggage will stop free-flowing energy and instead create blockages, exhaustion, and frustration.

Having stagnant energy in your business or money energy centre is like having a giant boulder in the river of money that blocks the flow of money to your bank account and prevents a magical abundance experience in your life.

Everything becomes stressful, hard work, draining and you can feel depleted or unfulfilled.

Clutter is often a suggestion that you have unfinished business. It's a reflection of the 'stuck' or 'blocked' energy in your life.

The way to recognised emotional clutter around money is to look at your bank balance.

Is your bank balance lower than you need or want it to be? If the answer is yes... then you probably have some clutter around this subject that needs clearing.

I also love this chapter and money block clearing activity because it is so simple and free!

It only takes a small amount of time to clear clutter... you can start small and move onto bigger and better projects.

Once you have cleared the clutter:

1. Your business will be more vibrant and magnetic.

When you create order and harmony in your business,

your goals will be easier to reach. The circulation of life force energy will flow freely and attract abundance.

Clearing clutter removes blocks and imbalances from your workspace. When you inhabit spaces that are lit up with fresh energy, inspiration strikes and the most magnetic parts of your work personality can come to life.

2. You can improve your time management.

When you aren't feeling overwhelmed from the disorder in your business, you'll have more time to get quality work done. Not having to spend an hour finding a price list or tracking down your portfolio saves incredible amounts of time, too.

3. Open up to new possibilities.

When you clear away the clutter, you're allowing yourself to take bigger, more creative risks because you're no longer spending time and energy focusing on passed problems.

4. You'll know who to forgive.

When you empty a physical desk drawer, you can uncover some deep emotional blocks around money. Bad memories about a money venture gone wrong or a financial dream that couldn't actualise in your physical experience could start to materialise in your emotions.

Every bad memory that you 'confront' and 'de-clutter' or 'forgive', creates more room for the magical new goals on your dream board to become a reality.

I remember I had a desk chair that was donated to me by a business partner who had very bad morals around money. Every time I got to my desk to sit down, I was reminded of the negativity of this person. One of the best 'updates' I made was to donate the chair to charity.

5. Your habits will be highlighted.

There are many symbols in our lives that trigger habits. Some of these trigger bad habits. By clearing away something that has been bugging you or reminds you of a bad time in your life or a broken dream you can remove the trigger and open up space in your world for good habits. There is more about this in chapter 9 - ALTERNATIVES and good HABITS

6. Improve your sleep patterns.

When you clear out the clutter in your business, it can be easier to fall asleep and stay asleep. If you have done the work of de-cluttering your goals and money blocks you can 'rest easy' knowing you are on the right path to true, sustainable abundance.

And the bonus is that when you have slept well, you are more productive and better able to achieve your abundance goals.

7. You'll be better at problem-solving.
When your conscious and subconscious mind is free from blocks it's much easier to see the solution to any problem.

8. You will remove money blocks to abundance.

One of the instant benefits of de-cluttering is finding money ...sometimes 'actual money' and sometimes we find things that we had forgotten we had that are now useful and that will save us money.

I remember a time recently when I was de-cluttering and needed to shred some client documents that were no longer needed but which contained sensitive information. I looked up local shredding companies on the internet and asked around for some prices.

I happened to be clearing out a store cupboard that weekend and found my old 'paper shredder'. I had completely forgotten about this little machine.
Not only did I get rid of a lot of paper in a short amount of time but I found an appliance that could help me save money in the future.

9. You'll feel more confident and trust your instincts.

When it comes to making big decisions and trusting your instincts, clearing out physical spaces and emotional ones can ensure you 'feel' clearly. You will then be able to act with certainty, saving time and avoiding costly mistakes.

I talk about this in more detail in other chapters of the book. When you are not sure about something, and you've written up your 'pro's' and 'con's' lists and you have sought the right advice from the right people and yet you are still 'not sure', then this is your intuition telling you to 'hold fire', some thing's not right and you need to 'clear some clutter' in order to create space to 'think' and 'feel' clearly on the subject.

We are often pushed to make choices by circumstances or people... but I strongly suggest that you hold off deciding until you have cleared the clutter and removed the blocks.

10. You'll get an automatic bonus

There's no downside to de-cluttering. Everything will improve in every way. You'll feel fantastic, emotionally lighter, dynamic, and energised. Money and abundance will flow easier into your life.

Everything will be easier and more fun.

Tackling even a small problem will immediately help you feel lighter, brighter and more magical!

CHAPTER 8 - VISUALISATION

There is nothing your subconscious mind likes more than a clearly defined goal that it can really sink its teeth into. I mentioned earlier that the subconscious mind is powerful but we need to speak to it in its 'preferred language'. It doesn't understand 'words' in the traditional sense.

Visualisation is the key to unlocking your super-power and your potential. Your subconscious gets right up close and personal with your visualisations. You are finally 'speaking it's language'. Your subconscious loves to support you and feels happy and motivated to do so, but you need to learn its language and help it to 'get there'.

When the subconscious mind sees your visualisation of money in the bank and it knows that there is no money in the bank, it does what it can to prove your visualisation correct.

It is hard wired to resolve the conflict between where you are and what you have visualised.

The vision you create activates your creativity and motivation. You will suddenly find yourself doing things you would normally not consider doing, in an effort to achieve your goals.

I have mentioned before that I am not a psychiatrist and I have no degrees in working with the brain but I do have money in the bank and a roof over my head that are all the 'physical proof' I need to know that this is how the subconscious mind works.

Along with the AXIS PRACTICE, a daily practice of VISUALISATION is vital to achieve your goals.

I also recommend that you bring visualisation into your daily routine. It will then be easier to remember to do it and it will help you achieve your goals with greater speed.

So if you do the AXIS PRACTICE whilst you are just waking up, before your head has even left your pillow, then consider practicing your VISUALISATION whilst you are brushing your teeth or making your bed, your morning cup of coffee or breakfast. Instead of allowing your head to fill with thoughts of what you need to achieve that day, put 'yourself first' for once and think about 'your goals'.

I'm reminded at this moment about the 'air masks' on an aeroplane, I tell my mum this often too. Air hostesses or cabin crew (to be politically correct) have been telling us for years: 'Put your own mask on first before you try to help others'. You will be much more effective when you do. My mum was often the first to get up in our home but the last to be dressed and ready. She would run around organising the whole family and put herself last. If you can, turn this on it's head and put yourself first so that you become more effective.

I understand that it takes 2 weeks to form a habit. This might seem like a drag if you are as impatient as I am, but think for a moment about the bigger picture:

2 weeks versus a lifetime of wealth or poverty... Suddenly 2 weeks seems like a small sacrifice to make to achieve great things... do you agree?

I can pretty much guarantee that if you get into the habit of visualising your goals every day, twice a day at set times, the goal will start to materialise in what will feel like 'no time at all'.

You have to write down your goal in great detail first. Write down what your ideal day looks like once you have achieved your goal. Then imagine it. Then summarise it into a few bullet points or a couple of paragraphs or photographs (if you are a visual person like me) that you can read out loud. Or imagine whilst brushing your teeth or taking a shower/bath etc.

When I was manifesting £50,000 into my bank account I would have visions of myself walking along a gold pathway, I could feel the coolness of the gold metal beneath my feet, I could see that I was surrounded by fabulous gold light. To me, the smell of gold smells like and orange blossom (not sure why) but I could see and smell little pale flowers to my left and right as I walked along my gold pathway. I also imagined I was wearing a red and gold coat. I am not sure why this was significant perhaps red and gold coats are prevalent in story books and wealthy princes and princesses wear them. But that was what I imagined, so I went with it.

I also felt invincible on my golden path, it seemed that at any moment my red coat would turn into a super hero cape and I could be, or do, or have anything I wanted. The amount of '£50,000' would appear in my bank account whilst I was walking down my gold path.

Once I had finished imagining this goal, I would switch back to my daily routine of getting to the office, dealing with emails and clients and 'kind of' forget about the goal.

I started to notice that things would appear in my in-box or people would say something that would seem magical and important and I started to gather information and 'follow the bread crumbs' to achieve the goal.

It was like I was suddenly 'tuned in' to recognise the resources I would need to achieve my goals. It felt like the right people and things were being drawn toward me. I also felt inspired to take a few risks that I wouldn't normally take.
Every person's imagination is different and I urge you

to come up with a visualisation of what your life will be like when you have achieved your goal. Include sounds, smells, tastes, emotions, sensations. They all work together to create the most powerful end result. There is a helpful step-by-step guide at the end of this chapter.

The more passion and excitement you include in your visualisation, the faster and easier it will be to actualise.

Here comes the rub!
The reason why so many people believe that their dream boards don't work, visualisation is a load of 'old cow turd' and 'spiritual mambo jumbo is for the birds' is because:

The vision of your achieved goal is so beautiful and magical and when you are faced later that same day with a problem with excessively low vibrational energy the difference between how great you felt that morning and how awful you feel during the 'tricky moment' is so great that it can knock you off your axis.

That is why I wrote about the 'axis practice' first and then about visualisation later in the book. Once you are well versed in the 'axis practice', it will be easier to dust yourself off, untangle yourself from the tricky client's negative onslaught, remove the 'icky stickiness' of the low vibrational 'problem' from your experience and get back on with the business of attaining your goals.

When you practice the 'axis practice', the divide won't feel so overwhelming.
Being 'so sensitive', I personally used to feel the divide

in 'living 3D colour'. It would feel like I was made of glass and the tricky client could shatter me with a harsh glance or word. I would spiral out of control and it would take me so long to put myself back together again that I would actively 'give up' on my goals and wallow in self pity for weeks afterwards.

I would say things to myself like:
'that's what I get for trying'
'I need to stop dreaming so big'
'I am kidding myself if I think for one minute that I am able to attain these goals'... etc.

The reality is, we are on this beautiful planet to learn and grow. We need the 'icky sticky' drama of problem clients to help us grow. But how you deal with the 'nastiness' is the growth part. Take your deep breaths, do the 'axis practice' and you will feel so much better in no time.

If you work in a public space, where others can see you sitting at your desk, you can always excuse yourself and go to your car or the bathroom and practice your breathing there. Get yourself grounded and come back swinging!

Here are some useful tips for creating a LARGE visualisation goal:

STEP ONE

Sit quietly in a safe calm place and imagine you are in your own television series. It's all about you and your

wealth creation and the possibilities are endless.
You can have as many series or episodes as you like.

The television series might be called: 'your name''s
wealth and abundance journey'.

Start off with imagining in as much detail your success.
The type of day you are having. Think about the clothes
you wear, the way you look but more importantly the
way you feel on an emotional level. See yourself living
the life you dream of.

Add in sounds you hear, how things feel to touch, what
things taste and smell like.

If it's a brand new car you are dreaming of inventing,
think of that new car smell when you open the door
and how thick the steering wheel feels beneath your
fingers. The sound of the door closing and the 'click'
of the seatbelt. Feel the excitement in the pit of your
stomach when you turn the key and the engine 'roars'
into life. Your rear view mirror shows how bright, clear
and focused your eyes are, you can taste the freedom,
you feel epic, in control of your destiny. You can invite
anyone on the journey with you... you can drive to any
destination... you are in charge of your best life.

You are in the drivers seat and the editors seat. You get
to 'cut', 'take two' or delete anything that doesn't feel
absolutely perfect and magical.

Are you a sculptor that feels the clay squelch between
your fingers, you can hear the turning wheel humming

along as you sculpt and bend the clay to your will.

Are you the director of a huge firm that has staff running around doing your every bidding?

Or do you own your own farm and you wake up every day and care for the animals or the crops. Do you make your own jams and sell them at the market each weekend.

Do you own a clothing company and you imagine yourself hiring the models to walk down the runway with your exclusive range of clothing.

What if you are a baker and you get up early each morning and switch on the ovens, feel the heat pumping out of the kitchen and smell the delicious freshly baked bread or cakes.

Think of each step of your day and how awesome you feel living your best life. Your days are magical, your inventions are loved by everyone and you are wealthy beyond your dreams.

STEP TWO

Imagine now that you are watching this television programme as a hologram and you can step right into the hologram and it becomes your reality.

When you step into it, the pixels that make up the hologram turn into tiny little rainbow coloured, organic molecules that are easily absorbed through your skin and into your blood stream, they become a wonderful magical part of your actual every day living experience.

The colours, smells, images are all absorbed through your skin. The television series is effectively a part of you. The visualisation is now coursing through your veins. You are the wealthy 'sculptor', 'farmer', 'clothing designer', going about your day. You are able to incorporate everything into every cell of your body.

Things magically align for you and everything flows perfectly.

STEP THREE

Open your eyes and come back to reality and go about your normal daily routine, safe in the knowledge that you have absorbed your visualisation, your subconscious mind knows exactly what to do to get you to this fabulous life.

It knows how to shorten the divide of where you are now and where you are in your visualisation.

STEP FOUR

Whilst you are getting used to doing visualisation, I recommend that you print out a few bullet points on a piece of paper or print out a photo graph or draw a symbol that reminds you of the visualisation and put these on your bathroom mirror or in your wallet or on your phone to remind you to start doing them. You could also put them in your electronic diary with a reminder to do them every morning.

They shouldn't take longer than five minutes. I eventually got so good at mine that I can do them whilst doing the other everyday chores that need doing.

Not driving of course, or not whilst operating machinery or a hot stove. But other things that don't take up much head space.

If you find yourself waiting for a client or forced to take a break because the internet is down etc, this is a great opportunity to get your visualisation going.

CHAPTER 9 - ALTERNATIVES

Reasons why we have an 'achilles heals' or 'habits'.

Our brains are actually wired to subsume a lot of the daily things we need to do in order to free up other parts of the brain which can then focus on interesting or important projects.

By eating the same breakfast everyday or following a certain routine to get dressed and ready for the day, we take a lot of decision-making out of the equation.

It means we can be thinking about something else, whilst we are on 'auto pilot' to get the boring chores done.

In order to change our habits we need to embrace 'alternatives'. Alternatives are the key to making lasting change.

Taking control of your habits and changing them is very

powerful. Because these habits accumulate day after day into outcomes that can be very significant.

If you have a bad habit around money, list the alternative habits now on a piece of paper or in your journal.

The psychology of the situation

The reason some of our habits around money exist, is because we have a fear of the alternative.

So, if for example you don't enjoy looking at your bank balance every day, this could be because it reminds you that you don't have enough money in it (fear).

Some of the people in our 'MONEY INSIGHTS' group immediately respond with 'they don't want to be burdened with looking at the bank balance every day, they feel it is extreme to have to do this every single day'.

My suggestion to them then, is that they have not really understood the alternative.

This is a habit that needs to change because if you don't look at your bank balance regularly and you don't count how much money is coming in every day, you will be out of touch with the reality of your financial situation. Plus your subconscious will get lazy, it won't help you take action to get you earning more money.

The outcome of 'not' looking at your bank balance

every day would be that you don't see the 'iceburg' below the surface and you carry on steering your ship into a disaster... end up bankrupt and going out of business!

Would you rather face your small fear today of looking at your bank balance and doing something about it? Or
Would you like to face a massive fear of going bankrupt and admitting to yourself and others that you didn't make it?

Can you agree with me now that 'facing your fear' of looking at the bank balance is a great option? We should be grateful that we have this option available.

If you have a bad habit think of the alternatives!

Is the frustration of living without the abundance of wealth you deserve not worth breaking your bad habit?

If you want to change your perspective think of the consequences of your actions.

Create a list of alternatives.

List all the things you can do to create more wealth, grow your business, brand, service or product.

CHAPTER 10 - RESPONSIBILITY

You are totally responsible for your life and your financial wealth. It is all up to you to make it happen.

You must embrace this fact if you want any kind of success in achieving your abundance and financial goals.

If you are playing the 'blame game', and telling yourself that every problem in your life is there because of 'some one else's action' you are not going to get very far at all.

Failure is always a result of the choices you yourself make... 'own them' and move on!

Only you can be in the driving seat. Only you can connect with your higher self and only you can determine what will make your life great.

If you fail to take responsibility for your wealth and abundance. And if you fail to guide yourself toward your dreams you will be setting yourself up for failure. You will be miserable.

It's easy to make excuses about your choices in life. I encourage you instead, to 'own the mistakes' you have made and 'forgive yourself' for them. Learn from them and grow.

People who take complete responsibility for their lives experience joy and happiness. They are in control of their destiny because they understand that they are responsible for their choices.

When we live every day as if it matters and everything we do matters we can create our best life. Every action you take affects your progress in one way or another. You are the one that makes a difference in your life. Let that difference mean that you share your voice with the world and help turn dark into light.

Energy follows thought.

"We become what we think about most."
Earl Nightingale's summation of the power of your thoughts is one of the most significant statements ever made.

If you consider the concept that your thoughts are always with you. They play themselves over and over again in your mind. They have your full attention most of the time and if they support you, you can easily achieve the life you have been dreaming of.
So take responsibility for your thoughts. If they are

negative in any way about any subject then its your
responsibility to find a 'pattern interrupter'.'

I find it helpful to turn it into a game. If I find my mind
wondering down a mental 'rabbit hole', I start to think
of a creative way to bring it back to focus on my goals.

EXAMPLE:

I was thinking about an upcoming 'new client' meeting
the other day. Not long afterwards, my mind started
to wander into a negative pattern of fear. It started to
throw up some negative ideas, suggesting that the
meeting wouldn't go well, I wouldn't be able to answer
questions 'off the cuff'... etc

I had to remind myself to stop that negative self talk
immediately and instead, 'set the intention' that the
meeting would go well.

I decided to take it a step further and I practiced a
visualisation exercise from chapter 8 - VISUALISATION
where the meeting went incredibly well. The client was
impressed with everything I said and I won the business.

The important thing to remember is that I took
responsibility for the actions. Both the original 'fear
actions', I 'owned' them and 'controlled' them and then
turned the outcome on its head in my minds eye.

And guess what... that's right, I won the business!

Henry Ford said: *Whether you think you can, or you*

think you can't–you're right.'

Energy follows your thought and your thoughts become actions. You are responsible for both your thoughts and your actions.

In chapter 1 of this book I outline the place I found myself in when my whole world was falling apart. It was really tough to admit to myself and everyone else that it was my own fault that I ended up in that particular big, black, dark, 'bear trap' hole.

I had no one else to blame but myself. I had ignored my instincts, I was the one that gave my power away, no one else had control of my power. It was all my fault.

When I considered the possible future of negativity: 'no control of my life' and spending my life living what 'someone else wanted for me', it felt like no future at all.

Is it not better to admit defeat, dust yourself off and get back on that horse!

Learn from your mistakes and lead your horse down a different path. A path to a life of wealth, abundance, happiness and joy.

I know it is difficult to imagine a great life when you are surrounded by the darkness of a black hole. But I am living proof that it can be done. If I can do it, so can you!

CHAPTER 11 - TRUTH

When we speak or act or live 'our truth' the magic really starts to happen.

Have you ever been drawn to a speaker because what the person was saying rang true for you?
It hit a cord within you, sparked interest and you wanted to find out more. This is when someone is 'speaking their truth'. I often get goosebumps when this happens.

'Speaking' or 'living your truth' means that you are living and acting with 'integrity'. When we do the 'Axis Practice' in the morning, we are invoking our 'higher selves' or our 'true selves' to be fully embodied with us throughout our day. By doing this, we are far more likely to ask for what we want and need from the world around us, and we will start to 'live our truth'. Because we are 'living our truth', life tends to flow better. Life is nicer, we are living in the 'zone'.

When we are in the 'zone', we don't settle for second

best. When you invoke your 'higher nature' you are taking 'inspired action' toward living in harmony with your personal goals and values.

There is a belief system that suggests that before we come to this planet, we have a set of ideas that we need to achieve and goals to actualise in order to complete our journey in this lifetime.

If we don't complete these during our lifetime, we may need to come back and try again. Your higher self is in charge of these ideas and goals, it holds the 'bigger picture' of that energetic part of you that is in constant contact with your 'Divine Soul'. When you listen to it and align with it, your goals are easier to co-ordinate for this and other lifetimes.

If you align with your higher self every day, you will have a clearer signal or stronger communication as to what you need to do and achieve each and everyday.

The way to know if you are connected with your higher self and your goals and intentions is the way you feel.

Your 'gut instincts' are an indicator as to where you are in terms of your goals. If you feel amazing, bright, shiny, perfect and magical, then you are on the right track.

If, however, your gut tells you that something is wrong, you feel, uncomfortable, listless, down, 'out of sorts' then you are not on the right path or journey.

The reason some of us step off of our true path in the

first place is often to do with a very real and immediate conflict that we might face when we want to choose our own path.

If our chosen path conflicts with someone else's path, 'who' or 'what we are' and 'how' or 'where we should spend our time' doesn't align with theirs.

Which is fine if you don't need this person in your life, if it's easy to part ways with them, but what if you are a child and they are your primary caregiver?

If you rely on this person for food, shelter and warmth, it can be very difficult to confront them. And if they have a very strong personality and determination to keep to their path, you may be swept up into their way of doing things, caught up in their daily agendas and their life's journey.

Even when we are adults, conflict can be scary for a sensitive person. I have spent most of my life avoiding conflict. I will sacrifice a lot before I face or confront someone. That is how I ended up in the 'rabbit hole' that I describe in the first chapter of this book.

I did not trust my instincts, I did not follow my truth, I allowed others to tell me 'who', 'what', 'where', 'why' and 'when' I could 'be'... and I was miserable!

It takes a lot of courage to face the conflict induced by others. If they are not sensitive souls they may come on too strong and make us feel small and insignificant, powerless and worthless.

In business this can and does happen. Once again as sensitive people we need to make a conscious choice to follow our 'higher self' and 'act out our truth'. It does seem to be harder for sensitive people to do this, I know because I lived it. But I can say with my hand on my heart that if you do, you will be so much better for it.

"Life shrinks or expands in proportion to one's courage."
Anais Nin

Face the fear and do it anyway. If you follow the instructions outlined in this book you can confidently let go of bad business relationships and know that you will be better off for it because I have given you great tips to attract new, higher vibrational clients.

Download the meditation at
www.abundance-magic.co.uk/moneyvane

If you are hanging around with low vibrational clients, your business will suffer. If you take brave steps to remove these negative relationships from your life, your business will start to thrive.

Download the meditation at
www.abundance-magic.co.uk/fearless

For example:

I had a client who I had worked with for about a year. He was impressed with the work we were doing and we had a monthly meeting to talk about the next marketing strategy. For one of the campaigns, he wanted to latch onto the concept and ride the coat tales of a world famous brand.

He was determined to copy a well known brand's icon and use it in his latest leaflet designs. I told the client that unfortunately it would be illegal to do this and that because this brand had so much power and money behind it, they would easily be able to sue him for using their icon as part of his marketing campaign.

He made it crystal clear in the meeting, in front of his colleagues (witnesses) that I should take the fall for the copying of the icon... 'if it came to it'.

The conundrum:
If I took the risk of copying the work then I would be able to continue working with the client and my contract with him would continue. I knew instinctively that if I said I was not prepared to take the fall, then he and I would have to part ways.

I had a choice to make.

I decided to trust my instincts, and follow my principles. It was more than just the money that was at stake!

It was also about my values, who I am, what my business journey is about. Am I the type of person who bends or breaks the rules in business, marketing and branding?

I wrote a very nice email to the client explaining my stance on the subject. I had decided that I would not be able to take part in the design of this particular marketing campaign.

I fully expected and anticipated his reply, which came through shortly after I hit send. He had decided that he would no longer be working with me and that his business would be going in a different direction.

I cannot describe the relief I felt when I received his email. I actually had a physical reaction, I jumped up out of my chair punched the air and exclaimed: YESSSSS!!!!!

Although I was losing a client and therefore money in the bank, the amount of time and stress this client was causing me by being in a 'different place' and on a 'different journey' to me was just not worth the effort or the money.

I was so relieved that I even did the 'funky chicken dance of joy' to celebrate. Luckily, I was alone at the time, because let's face it, there are some things that the world is better off not seeing. It is not a graceful, dance in any way, shape or form.

PHYSICAL SOLUTION

We often adopt the truth of others from early on in our childhood. As sensitive people we can see how upset family members get when 'their way' is not adhered to.

When we decide to 'speak our truth', we may have a whole 'life-time' of 'giving up our truth' to contend with.

Scary right? Years and years of making ourselves small so that other's needs could be met. It's difficult to turn this thought process around and start living our most 'authentic life'.

To make the switch and face conflicting with others we need to learn to sometimes say 'NO'.

I know this can be terrifying for a sensitive person.

I have met some sensitive people that are so scared of conflict, that they will actually lie and say the word 'YES' to the client but then they cannot commit to complete the task because the work they will be doing goes against their 'authentic self'.

This is an incredibly unhealthy and unhelpful place to be for both the client and the sensitive supplier.

The client heard the words 'YES' so is expecting their wish to be actualised and the sensitive person is like a 'deer caught in the headlights', they cannot move forward.

It would be far better for everyone if the sensitive person could learn to use the word 'NO' from time to time. However, the word 'NO 'can be a negatively charged word which invokes feelings like guilt, shame and fear.

A sensitive person has spent their whole life in service to others and the concept of doing something for themselves, or something other than what has been requested of them, can raise all kinds of feelings of guilt and panic... are they letting someone down? Is it allowed?

To make the transition easier for sensitive people, I suggest that you find ways of saying 'NO' that are 'gentle' but 'effective'.

Example:
Instead of saying a point blank 'NO' to a client, perhaps use words like: 'I will look into it for you'
or 'I like that idea, but I need to make sure it can be done'

This takes the drama out of the moment and allows the client to take a back seat because they have been assured that they will get an answer. If the client is headstrong, it helps them feel like they have been listened to and understood. It makes them feel like they have done their job, now it's over to the supplier to do the rest.

This also affords the sensitive supplier some much needed space and time to gather their thoughts and decide how they want to proceed. They can then take their time to either find someone else to do the work or spend some time working out how to solve the client's problem without compromising their own truth.

If the sensitive person has been raised to always be good, always do as they are told, they need to find a way to 'resolve this conflict' within themselves in order to 'live their truth', bring their prodigious skills and gifts to the world and create a magical, sustainable business that thrives.

They need to find a way to be less 'judgy' of themselves, less critical and less apologetic. Think about the concept that is 'self sabotage'. If you continue to hurt yourself in order to not get hurt by others, it can only end badly!

I encourage you to embrace your most magical self.

You may think you are not perfect enough, it doesn't matter, because I believe in you, I think you are perfect and your higher self thinks you are perfect too. That is 'two against one', by the way!

If you connect with your higher self every day via the 'Axis Practice' you will start to get the message that you are exactly right, you are a wonderful, amazing magical co-creator that is ready to share their wonderful gifts with the world.

It doesn't matter where you are in your journey of self discovery, the only thing that matters is that you start today, 'right here' and 'now', make the conscious choice to align with your truth, let go of the past, let go of the reasons why you were not aligned with your 'true self', embrace your 'higher self' and move forward from this day onwards.

Promise yourself that you will only be true to your own goals, your principles and your specific wisdom and truth.

METAPHYSICAL HEALING

If you have a meeting coming up with a client and you are worried about fluffing the whole thing, or you are worried you won't be able to say 'NO' we have developed a lovely meditation that you can practice before you even get there.

This is also a great meditation to help you when you need to feel grounded and want to set the intention that your day or meeting will go well:

www.abundance-magic.co.uk/meetingspace

PHYSICAL SOLUTIONS TO LIVING YOUR TRUTH

1. Take responsibility
As we outlined in Chapter 10, this is your life and you are in control. You may have had to adapt to others when you were a child but that part of your life is over now. You are in the drivers seat and it's your responsibility to own: 'who', 'what', 'where' 'why' and 'when' you are. You are in control of what you 'see', 'hear', 'touch', 'say'. Don't let clients or staff take advantage of you! Ask for help if you need it.
Learn to say 'NO' in the nicest way possible.

2. Focus and determination
Instead of spending your time avoiding conflict, focus your energy instead on getting from where you are to where you want to be. Create and communicate boundaries to yourself and clients.

3. Positive self-talk
Let go of any negative self talk that no longer serves you. Get a pattern interrupter if you need one.

4. Embrace courage and authenticity
I have mentioned your 'Higher-Self' throughout this book, I want to mention at this point, your 'inner child'. Your 'inner child' is an integral part of you and if you speak up authentically you are acknowledging and embracing that part of yourself. This is important because your 'inner child', like your subconscious is a great tool to use to achieve your goals.

Your 'inner child' lights up when you pat yourself on the back, when you 'high five' your business partner. It is the playful, deep part of you that holds all of your first experiences and childhood memories. This is where your beliefs are imprinted. It is also what makes us different from others.

Every time you authentically and courageously speak up, you love yourself a little bit more and your 'inner child' beams with glee and delight. It may sound cheesy and weird, it may defy your steely, adult determination to take yourself seriously. But if you please your 'inner child' you will be acknowledging your true self on a very deep level and you will start to experience the rewards.

You have an inherent right to be heard, valued, and respected. Your 'inner child' knows this and wants this first and foremost. If you deny yourself these things, you can suffer the consequences of an embarrassing temper tantrum!

A 'CATEGORY 5' TEMPER TANTRUM

There are times when we are going about our busy days, getting projects completed, meeting the client brief and then suddenly something triggers us on a very deep level. This can bring up intense feelings of debilitating pain. This can cause us to lose our 'adult logic' and instead of behaving like a grown up, a stable, healthy and empowered person, we find ourselves in the throws of a 'category 5' temper tantrum.

I have only lost my temper 3 times in my life. It is quite an unnerving experience and not one that I ever wish to relive again. A temper tantrum is your 'inner child's' way of crying out for help. It raises problems that need your time and attention to heal.

One of my funny (now it's funny) memories is of a temper tantrum I threw when I was employed by a rather infuriating bully.

The bully I was working for had been pushing my buttons for about 3 years. He only employed women and there was always one of them in his office crying about something he had said to them.

The bully, let's call him 'Adam', tried many things to get me to cry too, but all his attempts failed. I have never been able to cry easily and I hadn't even realised at the time that he was doing it on purpose.

I was in my early 20's, I was quite 'girly' looking... with long, blond hair and a million freckles that covered my face, no matter how much sun cream or make-up I applied. These attributes made me appear quite innocent and fragile.

I, however, have always taken myself very seriously and I expected the rest of the world to do so too. I'm sure I looked like a complete push-over. I am sensitive, which bullies pick up on straight away. But I have always been very focused and driven when it comes to my career and work in general. I have always dedicated every working hour to further my career and improve my prospects. I always arrive early, I always do what it takes to get the job done!

I was also raised by an 'A-type' personality mum who never, ever held back. I was quite used to 'loud opinions', they didn't frighten me the way they did the other women I worked with. I had embraced the chaos of the bully's work place working my way up from graphic designer to manager and I was even one of the company directors.

As much as Adam was a bully on one hand, he would also do what was necessary to improve and grow his business. He recognised my hard work and dedication and promoted me over the years. His bullying was annoying, but I always managed to keep my cool within the confines of the office walls. I would calm myself down when I got home and rest and recharge, prepared for the following day's onslaught.

I rationalised Adam's behaviour, sometimes even feeling sorry for him, I pitied his lack of compassion and that he wasn't able to communicate in an evolved manner. I also recognised that he was a good business man and he had grown his company from 1 employee to 21 employees. Skills not to be sniffed at! On some level I was really impressed with his efforts. I also felt like I was learning a lot from him.

Adam was always super challenging with me on a one-to-one basis, I coped well with all his digs and his over assertive behaviour. I took on board the good bits of information and ignored the rest. However, one day Adam went too far. This time he undermined me in front of my team.

I was known for being calm under pressure and the person my 'hand-picked' team turned to for guidance, help and support. I was voted 'manager of the year' every year and I felt I had earned their respect.

Undermining me in front of my team reminded me of the many times in my childhood when I had been undermined in front of my siblings. Chauvinism was rife in those days and I was often picked on for being female. If one of my brothers made a mess, I was told that because I'm female, I should clean it up. I was never invited on camping trips, because it was 'boys only' etc. It was incredibly degrading, hurtful and infuriating.

It brought up what felt like a lifetime of anger, frustration and indignation. My inner child threw the biggest temper tantrum of my life. I felt the heat rush up through my entire body, it felt like my skin was prickling, on fire. I exploded!

I used all the 'big' words I could think of, ranting out a string of expletives, aimed directly at Adam's face, in front of everyone!

I'm blushing now as I remember the extent of the fit I threw and the words I used. Yes, me, who never swears, such language, I had no idea I even had it in me.

Then my mind went blank, the office walls were closing in on me. I had to get out. I stormed out of the office, slamming the door behind me. The glass trembled in its frame, I'm surprised it didn't break. I went to the car park to calm down, my legs weren't sturdy enough to hold me, I had to crouch down and lean against my car.

I remember thinking about all the bullying I had put up with over the years. All the late nights, the dedication, the blood sweat and tears that had gone into growing the business... and this was the thanks I got! This was the last straw! I wanted to resign immediately, without notice!

I had stormed out without my car keys and it slowly dawned on me that I couldn't get away to finish this weird trembling experience in the privacy of my own home.

In the time it took for me to get my breath back and stand up straight again, Adam had joined me in the car park. I was spitting mad and shaking with indignation. He spoke gently to me then, much more gently than I remember him speaking to anyone before, he calmed me down by apologising and asking me what exactly the problem was.

While Adam was apologising, I was rationalising that the outcome of this particular discussion was irrelevant, I had resigned myself to the fact that if he fired me or if I walked out here and now it wouldn't matter. I could drive off into the sunset and go and get another job with another company. Anything would be better than suffering the insult of being undermined in front of my team.

My 'inner child' drew a line in the sand that day. It decided that the way I was being treated was out of order. It would not tolerate this humiliation and it was prepared to sacrifice everything to make it's point.

Adam apologised enough for me to take him seriously and I ended up working there for another 3 years.

What this temper tantrum taught me:
I did some soul searching and research after that event. I discovered that our 'inner child' is responsible for cellular memory. The experiences that we go through as children are locked into each cell of our bodies which can later be triggered by a memory.

Your inner child, lives within you. It will never leave you. Your inner child will act out if you are not being true to yourself and to your life's objectives. And if you are being unfairly treated. In my example, I had been ignoring my inner child. Every bullying encounter over the years had been ignored, I had tried to focus on the bigger picture of my career, and had pushed my inner child's needs way down low. Instead of stopping, listening to my instincts and doing something about it, I had ignored the warning signs. If you have ever experienced an epic, adult temper tantrum like mine, this is the work of your 'inner child', letting you know that you have some deep seated issues to deal with.

When we lose ourselves to a tantrum, we get 'knocked off of our axis'. The good news is that when these wounds are raised to the surface, we can deal with them and heal them. It's also worth mentioning here that the other way these traumas actualise is through 'defensiveness'. If anyone tells you regularly, that you are being 'defensive', this is a warning for you to look introspectively, look a little closer at the problem. This issue goes a bit deeper. You could have some 'inner child' issues that you need to deal with.

Instead of getting angry with the people who are telling you that you are defensive, take some time to meditate on why your buttons are being pushed. Having the right tools to heal this trauma can lead you on to bigger and better things. It can also ensure that you stay grounded during your work day, no matter which bullies you encounter. I have since worked through the issues raised and spent some time forgiving and healing these past hurts.

If Adam tried to undermine me in front of anyone now, I would not react in the way he would expect. I would be clear of mind and thought. I would instead feel pity for him and hope that he can evolve so that he no longer needs to bully people to get them to do his bidding.

PHYSICAL SOLUTIONS

1. Ask yourself what is your pain or trauma really about. Think back to your childhood and see if you can remember a time when you felt this way. By having an awareness of the pain we can ensure we do not ignore the emotion.

Bring the feeling up to the surface to breathe high vibrational energy into it and forgive the person who caused the trauma or pain in the first place. Remember also to forgive yourself for any emotions you have around this feeling. There are deeper ways to heal if you would like to try a meditation.

Download the meditation at www.abundance-magic.co.uk/forgiveness

2. Acknowledge your inner child, thank it for bringing this problem and hurt feelings to your attention. Hug your inner child by bringing high vibrational energy up from the centre of the earth into your chakras. Never be afraid or feel cheesy about giving your inner child love and attention. No one needs to know you are doing it. It can be done in the privacy of your own mind.

3. Connecting your 'higher self' with your 'inner child' is another powerful way to show your 'inner child' that you acknowledge it's existence. This is a 'super power connection' that will help guide you throughout your wealth and abundance journey and improve the speed with which you achieve your goals. This is achieved by the 'AXIS PRACTICE' mentioned earlier.

4. Letting go of the past and leaving behind the negative memories, plus forgiving the trauma helps us to move to an altered state of improved perspective.

When you are in this 'altered state', you are functioning on a higher vibrational level and you will be more in tune with your 'higher self' and your 'inner child'. This is where the magic happens. In this state you will start to move mountains. Turn darkness into light. It can be scary, it is hard work, but it is worth it. You are worth it.

A mantra for healing:
Thank you for bringing this to light, I am sorry it happened, I love you, I forgive you, I have moved on.

METAPHYSICAL HEALING

Forgiveness is key.
Write down all the 'tricky' things in your life from your childhood or from your 'tricky' business experiences that still hold a charge. Anything that makes you feel angry or indignant.
If there is a story you tell people often, a story about indignation, bullying or when the world seemed 'unfair' then this is probably a good place to start.

Practice forgiving these people and experiences.

www.abundance-magic.co.uk/forgiveness

HOW IT WORKS

HOW THIS 'MONEY SYSTEM' WORKS

These oracle cards are based on asking the wonderful animals that we share this planet with for their inspiration to create abundance. We can learn a lot from animals, they are masters at adapting and manifesting and creating abundance for themselves.

They are constantly sending signals outwards and manifesting different things in their lives, they don't wake up everyday and complain (the way I have been known to) that they are too broke, too fat or too skinny, don't have the right job, having a bad hair day, their hair is too straight, not straight enough, not enough hair, they are not good enough, perfect enough, loved enough...the list goes on!

Instead they trust their instincts, they know what they need to do next to take care of themselves and their offspring. They know exactly who they are and what their divine purpose in life is. They don't have any doubts about who they are or what their next goal is, or, in fact, what they should do next.

Have you ever had a pet dog?

Have you noticed how they wake up everyday in a state of joy, they cannot wait to get going, they run around the house waking everyone up eager to embrace the delights of this precious new day. They look like they are bursting out of their skin with excitement and anticipation. I've noticed that it's only us humans that might lower the tone, bring them down a peg or two if we wake up in a less than jovial mood.

WHY ANIMALS?
I'm not sure if it's because I grew up in 'Sunny South Africa', surrounded by a myriad of weird and wonderful creatures, but I have always had a natural affinity with all animals, even 'creepy crawlies' I might not want a spider in my personal space but I won't kill them either.

I cannot count the times I have saved spiders from bath tubs and hand basins, even when others look at me mystified, why do I bother?
It feels a bit like I am part of the spider's destiny, I hold their future in my hands, I can help them and that energy comes back ten fold.

What you give out comes back to you, so why not give out good things. Instead of squishing the spider I can choose instead to help it on its way. And it doesn't stop there, I have been helping all kinds of creatures and strays my whole life. Much to my mum's complete and utter horror. She grew up in England and has no affinity with 'creepy crawlies'!

I might have inherited her love for larger animals though. She is naturally good with them and they all adore her. We always had animals in our home when I was growing up, we had a large garden and a variety of pets lived (sometimes peacefully) in the same 'space time continuum'.

I love the idea of co-creating with all the beautiful creatures in the world, channelling their energy and incorporating their wisdom in my quest to improve my financial situation.

We are so lucky to share this planet with a myriad of fascinating creatures. They have all evolved over time to survive and thrive in sometimes really harsh environments. I feel inspired by the tenacity of all creatures and moved by their determination to succeed against all odds. In our western lifestyle, we spend so much of our time indoors, cut off from the wondeful energies of mother nature and disconected from other living creatures.

By reconnecting with our true selves and starting to 'feel' the energy of nature all around us we can release blocks and find insights into how to improve our lives and ultimately our activate our own personal magic and abundance.

I created these cards to help myself with my money blocks and goal setting. I found that my subconscious brain likes to see symbols and pictures to help it focus on specific goals. An animal is the perfect symbol for my subconscious mind to make a link from 'where I am' to 'where I want to be'.

My subconscious brain likes to storys around animals that it can associate with, it turns the theory into a nice visual that my style of learning can more strongly associate with and agree with. It then makes it easier to achieve my goals. I can reason with my brain all day and it will ignore me, but show it a picture and tell it a story that accompanies the picture... and 'bam'! It finally understands what it needs to do, it understands the work ahead of it and supports me in my quest to achieve abundance and riches.

I recognise right now that all the lessons I have learned, all the experiences I have been through, throughout my life were leading up to this moment where I could amalgamate these little nuggets of information and combine them into the oracle card system 'MONEY INSIGHTS'

The way we reach the top of a mountain (a goal) is through a thousand tiny steps, and we have to break it down into small steps to achieve our goals. The lessons are therefor broken down into 1-3 subjects per week.

As I mentioned, my brain responds much better to a game or fun than dry, hard, boring rules.

Example:

If I'm told I have to phone 3 potential new customers today, my brain thinks of a million other things to do instead. Procrastination rules the day!
Whereas if it's suggested that I write down the fact that some money came into the business, I have no problem writing that down and when I'm writing down the sum of money, a special 'light energy' is activated within me and I'm suddenly inspired to get more of that feeling.

This results in me phoning around to see who needs more of our products or services, or if any of my clients would like to recommend me to their colleagues. simple, fun, rewarding...result!

I'm not being 'told' to do something 'dry' and 'boring', ...it circumvents that natural resistance to being 'ordered' to do something which 'feels' like a chore. It suddenly becomes a game to see how much more of this positive feeling I can get into my life right now, this minute!

If you purchased these cards and book, it could be the universes' or your subconscious mind's way of showing you how to approach your 'financial journey' in a different way. By looking at the bigger picture, thinking about all the things you need to do to achieve greatness and asking the animals that we share the world with, for their wisdom and insights to help you achieve your goals.

The reason the cards work so well for me, is because they show me what I most need to know and focus on right now, today! It removes the clutter and confusion and the hard work of not knowing where to start.

It is important to choose the cards with your non dominant hand, ie: with your left hand (if you are right handed) and vice versa. This is something to do with your subconscious picking out the cards for you to follow, it circumvents the strong frontal lobe (my control freak) part of the brain that always takes control of the situation and tries to bend everything to it's own will.

When I practiced Thai Chi I was awakened to the idea that it is better to 'work with the force of nature' and 'with your opponents energy' rather than try to 'stand in its way'. Rivers know this only too well too, its better to wind along and take an easier path and flow with nature rather than trying to force your way through rocks or over mountains.

Esther Hicks (www.abraham-hicks.com) in her teachings refers to the behaviour as 'upstream' trying to paddle upstream, instead of turning your boat into the down stream of the water and allowing gravity and the flow of water to help you achieve your goals.

Of course I totally understand that there is a time for 'force' and 'dynamite' and 'structure' and 'willpower'. We would not have roads, bridges or high-rise buildings and modern society would look very different without 'brute force' and 'dynamite'.

However, what I am saying is that if 'brute force' and 'willpower' has not brought in your money goals, if you have tried 'brute force' and your bank account is still nearly empty. Perhaps its time to try something else!

I believe the reason I felt so inspired to write and finish this book, is that it is aligned in many ways with what I really wanted to do with my life.

I remember being a teenager and wanting to spend everyday working on creative projects, it didn't matter to me if I was sculpting or painting or even designing furniture, provided it was an outlet for my creative juices. I embraced it wholly.

However, life got in the way, and well intentioned parents and teachers convinced me that there would be no money in 'creativity', they were terrified I would become a 'starving artist'. Being the sensitive person I am, meant that I could 'feel' their fear loud and clear. This set me back in life in some ways, however, everything happens for a reason.

I am not holding any grudges here, I just mention it because I am sure there are many of you out there reading this book that may have had similar experiences. Did someone close to you, important in your life during your formative years put fears into you about following your dreams?

Many of our friends and family try to control us without knowing it, they try to keep us small. They love their own negativity so much and they love sharing it with us. They are afraid that if we follow our dreams and it grows into something amazing and powerful. We will leave them behind, alone with their drama, we won't be there to commiserate with them and agree with how bad their lot in life is and they might feel abandoned and unsafe.

They don't do it on purpose, they don't consciously do it, however, you need to decide for yourself if you want to spend your life, all your beautiful days sitting around listening to the negative complaints from others, or do you want to soar through life, be all you can be... Be the bright, beautiful, positive, co-creator that you were destined to become?

One of the brilliant ways this money system works is that it will highlight blocks and tricky problems that you may not be aware of.

By pulling 3 new cards each week, your subconscious will help you identify and highlight which areas of your business or your personal life you need to focus on to move forward. And ultimately help you to create sustainable financial abundance.

Simplifying our goals, problems, blocks and self-sabotage by taking a look through they eyes of animals to see your challenges differently and help your human mind to refocus on what is truly important.

MOUSE

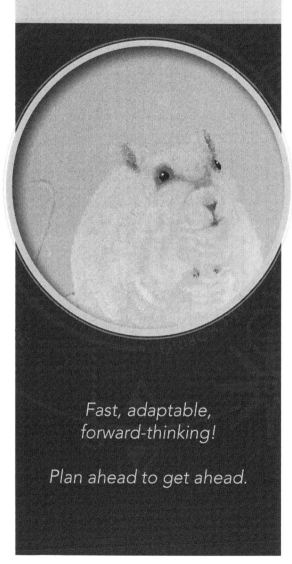

*Fast, adaptable,
forward-thinking!*

Plan ahead to get ahead.

1

MOUSE OR RAT

Let's face it, mice and rats have a bad reputation in the Western world.

They are not revered like they are in the Chinese culture. I think it's a shame that we don't honour the different animals the way our Eastern brothers and sisters do.

In their culture, the rat was the first to turn up for a meeting with Budha and therefore gained the first place out of 12 star signs. If you have picked this card you need to spend some time thinking about the way you show up for business.

Our Western minds should open and allow us to focus more on the benefits and positive traits of animals.

Rats are always early. I'm a rat (or, I should say, I was born in the year of the rat according to the Chinese horoscope system) which means that I have a built in compulsion to be early. I set reminders in my calendar and alarms on my phone to make sure I arrive early or on time. I spend about 5 minutes the day before any new business meeting, planning the event to make sure I know where I'm going, what I'll be wearing, and even what meals I need to prepare to ensure I arrive on time. (I have various food allergies so planning is essential)

'Plan ahead to get ahead' is the motto to take home from this wily creature. There are also no excuses in this day and age. Our phones have alarms and calendars can send us messages to remind us of important upcoming meetings. I include all my clients in my calendar so that they get the same reminders about the meeting that I do. This has saved countless hours of wasted travel time and ensures everyone is on the same page.

You never get a second chance to make a good first impression. So make sure you look smart and you are on time for business meetings. You need to take yourself seriously and show the universe that you mean business!

Make sure your shirt is ironed, your socks are clean and your shoes are polished. This is not rocket science people! If you take yourself seriously, the universe will too!

If you don't take yourself seriously, your clients won't and guess what? Neither will the universe or your subconscious. Failing to prepare is preparing to FAIL!

Arriving early or on time also puts you in a position of

control. You will have had a chance to set the scene, feel confident and relaxed, and deal with any problems that may have cropped up.

Add meetings to your calendar as soon as physically possible. I use 'Gmail's' calendar and it allows me to invite 'guests' to the meeting so that it's automatically in their calendar too.

It's worth mentioning that I used to get extremely annoyed when other people were late to meetings. It felt rude and annoying - like a personal insult.

I turned this to my advantage.

I invented a couple of coping strategies that helped me change my attitude about other people's tardiness. And ultimately improved my relationship with myself and money. Instead of being angry and feeling like it was a personal slight against me, I am now as calm, cool and collected as the next guy or girl during the meeting.

I coped by:

 A. Acknowledging that most people don't like to be late. So give them a break!

They may not have my powers of organisation and planning. I can guarantee that they are really good at something that I am not great at, so I keep this in mind. Getting stressed out about other peoples tardiness is a waste of my energy.

B. I always make sure I have some work with me that I can do when I arrive early.

- Checking my emails and even answering the easy ones, ensures I make the best of that time.
- I am constantly brainstorming ideas for different art and design projects, or thinking up new ways to market my businesses.
- I make sure I am able to capture any ideas, either on my phone or laptop.
- A mini meditation goes a long way to set the scene for the meeting. I set the intention that it's going to be a fantastic meeting, and guess what? It pretty much always is a FANTASTIC meeting!

MONEY INSIGHTS:

1. Show up on time for business and look the part!
2. Set alarms and reminders and get organised
3. Show up to win more business
4. Use your time well
5. Prepare for meetings 'Plan ahead to get ahead!'
6. Every evening set the intention that the following day is going to be a great day to make money!

TIGER

*Willpower, courage,
and personal strength!*

*The balancing forces
of yin and yang.*

2

TIGER

Decide what you really want. Tigers are associated with stealth, fierceness and strength. They know exactly what they want and stalk their prey relentlessly until they have it.

If you don't know what you want, it's really difficult to FIND IT, STALK IT and finally POSSESS IT.

It's even harder for the universe and your subconscious brain to help you achieve it. This idea is reflected in the behaviour of some people who sit around frustrated that they haven't won the lottery. And yet, they haven't even purchased a lottery ticket. They moan to their friends and family... if only they could win the lottery, all their problems would be solved.

The UK lottery company has recognised this strange behaviour and has come up with the clever advertising slogan: 'you have to be in it to win it.'

You have to decide what you want in this life and your clever subconscious brain will start to help you to achieve it. The interesting thing about your subconscious mind is that it has a tricky way of working.

Your subconscious cannot understand concepts in the traditional sense i.e. you can tell it all day long that you want to earn money and think of all the lovely things you could buy with the extra money and it won't make a bit of sense to your subconscious.

What will, however, make sense and be taken ON BOARD in big capital letters, are pictures, symbols, facts and practical lists.

That is why I came up with these cards in the first place.

If I see the symbol of the tiger, it jolts my subconscious reminding me what I really want.

There are many techniques to help you find out what you want, or rather how to earn the money in the first place.

Most people suggest that you should remember what you wanted to be when you were 5 or 15. What career path did you want to take. Did you see yourself as a business owner, scientist or artist?

I'm not talking about what your parents or grandparents suggested you become. My dad wanted me to be an accountant of all things. I used to sit in accountancy classes aged 12 - 13 dumbfounded that not one word was making any sense to me. I was easily able to get 'A's' in other subjects but nothing made sense in this subject. I recognise what a big and important role accounting plays in any business but it just did not make one bit of sense to me personally.

Happily my lack of accounting nous is not an issue these days because there are various amazing software packages available that can take care of it all.

The important thing is that your dream job or the work that you love to do, that is what you should be focused on, and leave accounting to the accountants.

How to recognise that you are doing what you are meant to be doing to earn money:

You will be super energised when you start doing the type of work you love doing. You'll wake up before the alarm goes off, you'll be excited to get to work. You will find anything that tears you away from this work annoying and something to be dealt with at top speed so that you can get back to doing what you love doing.

Work will feel like fun and guess what, you'll get paid to have fun. So what are you waiting for?

Break it down though, it's no good quitting your job and not having a pay cheque at the end of the month.

Start small with small wins. I started writing this book and painting the originals for these cards alongside my main business. I used my spare time carefully. Managing my energy, working in dates with friends and family around my painting.

I channelled my inner tiger. I recorded my thoughts about my book on my phone, during my morning jog. Then amalgamate them when I had time. I was multi-tasking: keeping fit and working at the same time.

Another great multi-tasking scenario was when I set up an art group which I called 'Art in the Attic'. It provided an opportunity to not only socialise with friends but also create beautiful, abundant paintings of animals and share laughter and joy with my friends at the same time.

My artistic friends also helped me 'hone' my style of painting. During the sessions I would ask all of them to tell me what they thought I could do differently with each painting. Over time I developed my painting style.

Think of ways that you can build in your new career or money making project around your existing life, take into consideration family needs too. Be creative. Instead of thinking of outings as time consuming interruptions, think of interesting and fun ways to spend time with your favourite people and earn a living too.

MONEY INSIGHTS:

1. Define what you would like to do to earn money
2. Create a vision board or dream board and update it regularly
3. List the steps you are going to take to move you toward your next goal

4. Stalk your prey relentlessly
5. Write your daily goals down every day
6. Follow the breadcrumbs

WORMS

Intelligent, capable, sensitive.

The ultimate in
recycling animal energy.

3

WORMS

Worms symbolise intelligence and being able to use your individual capabilities. Even without eyes, they can sense sunlight through their skin.

They are the ultimate in recycling animal energy.

My husband and I have a wormery. It is a great way to recycle kitchen scraps and, as we have an allotment, we use their waste product to fertilise the soil to grow fruit and vegetables for our kitchen. A never ending cycle.

Granted, when my husband first introduced a wormery to our home I was a bit squeamish about the idea. What if one escaped? The last thing I would want to deal with, but I soon realised the benefit of these lovely creatures.

They fit in with our lifestyle beautifully and I feel quite proud of the fact that we have less waste going into the council's waste system.

One of the worms' messages is to teach us to be self reliant. Have you heard the phrase 'you are stronger than you think you are' ?

Every now and then, someone will say these words to me, and I realise with embarrassment that they are right.

If you have pulled this card from the pack, it's the universe's way of telling you that you can do it. If you put your mind to it, you can achieve great things.

One of my blocks I had about my husband joining my branding business full time, and leaving his steady job with the company he had worked at for 30 years was the idea that we would struggle to get a mortgage in the future. Banks don't like to see is the word 'self employed' on their mortgage application forms.

Obviously this is a ridiculous notion. Millions of self employed people all around the world have mortgages. I had a mortgage before I met him and I was self employed then.

Whenever I draw the worm card, I remind myself of this story. I also know that I will always do what is necessary to make something work. If I have a new problem thrown at me from a client, or if I have a big bill to pay, I have always been able to solve the problem. I have always paid the bill.

Picking this card from the deck means that there may be something that has just come up that feels like a mountain to climb. I invite you now to turn it on it's head and make your mountain into a small molehill!...or at least lots of little molehills.

Break things down into bite size pieces. Our worms eat lots and lots of kitchen scraps but they don't eat it all in one go.

Practice is also so important. Practice makes perfect! Worm reminds us to keep going: 'keep on keeping on'.

The worm showing up is excellent, it is a sign that you are on the right track. Each problem you tuck into and work on improves you, makes you better, stronger, more focused. Embrace your problems and look inside yourself for the answers. You are strong enough.
You are talented enough. You do have what it takes to move forward and reach your goals.

MONEY INSIGHTS:

1. Break big problems down into smaller ones
2. You are stronger than you think you are
3. Embrace change and revel in the fact that you can do what you need to do

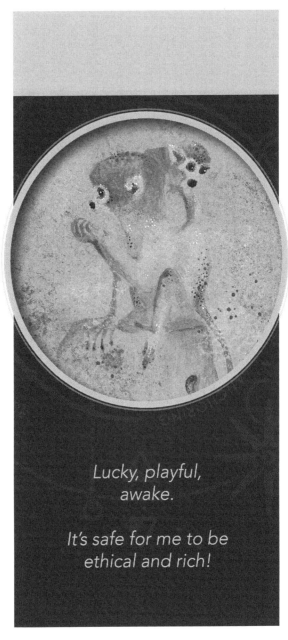

Lucky, playful,
awake.

It's safe for me to be
ethical and rich!

4

MONKEY

The monkey is a symbol of good luck. It represents a playful and lighthearted version of yourself. Awaken the 'inner child' in you.

Passive income.

Most people associate monkeys with playfulness.

They are the ideal animal to associate with if you want to feel free and playful, to enjoy life to the fullest, like a monkey, they don't sweat the small stuff. Life is for having fun, playing jokes on others and swinging from tree to tree, enjoying the bounty of fruit supplied by mother nature.

One of the best ways to create wealth is by earning a passive income. You can then start to feel a real sense of freedom and playfulness. It does take a lot of work up front and you do need to know which trees you are going to climb, but once you get to the top, you'll have more fun than a barrel of monkeys.

It takes bravery to swing from tree to tree in the beginning, but once you know you can trust that the branch is strong enough to hold your weight, your life will start to change for the better.

You do also need to clear any blocks you have around money, for example:

A: Choose your target market.
You may think that you need to be all things to all people, the antithesis to this is that there are 'riches in niches'. Choose a target market that you really want to work with.

Example:
I think most of my target audience for this book and these oracle cards will be sensitive souls, who love animals and who are spiritually minded. But most of all they are keen to start earning serious amounts of money.

I don't need to appeal to people who are already wealthy or who don't like oracle cards, or who are not interested in animals or people who think that this is just another 'woo woo' self help book. Some of my best friends would hate to have to pull three cards every week and focus on the animal messages, they would much rather pick up a very factual book and look at the facts and figures, research the subject in a professional way and get on with it.... end of!

This book and the cards and lessons are not for them.

Whoop! Be proud of the fact that you can narrow down your audience. Trying to be all things to all people results in being nothing to no one with zero sales.

B. Perfectionism.
Do you have to be perfect before you are successful? No, no, no... this message is specifically meant for all the control freaks out there. I am a self-confessed control freak. It was a big lesson for me to learn.

I had to start my first business because I was made redundant and no one was really hiring at the time. The country was in crisis, in the throes of a triple dip recession and I had to have money so I jumped feet first into running my own business.

Did I make mistakes? Yes, but guess what, I managed to pay my salary every month and I learned a lot along the way.

Believe me, I was nowhere near perfect when I started out. There is a great marketing book by Seth Godin who talks about 'shipping'. 'Shipping' in this context means getting things done. Get your products or services out to market, worry about perfecting them later. Stop procrastinating and get started. There will be time to perfect things along the way.

I cannot agree more. If I had waited until I was perfect before starting my business I would have been homeless. I'm going to bring in our monkey analogy right now too. Monkeys don't care if their hair is perfect or if they are overweight, or if they have the best house or best car, no, they get out there and go for it.

I started my branding business without a great website, I can design websites for other people fairly easily but for myself... aaaargh! It's the hardest thing in the world.

The problem is I like every colour, every style of design and every concept known to mankind. I couldn't see the wood for the trees.

Eventually I just started with a poor website and learned along the way that you need to change your website and marketing collateral all the time anyway, so just get on with it. People will forgive a poor website in the beginning. We all have to start somewhere.

C. Are you afraid people will think you are a fraud?

I know how real that fear is because I was literally shaking in my boots when I had my first new client meeting in a big boardroom with lots of faces staring back at me. I had to present my portfolio and myself to a room full of strangers.

But guess what, most people like to work with someone who is a bit humble and not over confident. Show the world who you really are, they might just love you!

It's worth thinking about the bigger picture at this point. Will anybody die if the meeting goes poorly?

Will anybody end up in hospital if you don't convince the client to go with your concept, or your big idea to promote their business?

No, of course not, but you have to get out there and test the branches, that's the only way you will learn what branches will hold your weight and what trees are best to climb. I eventually built up my portfolio and was finally able to build a website which showed off our work in the best light.

So get started!

Sure you may get a poor review, or some people might say untrue or hurtful things about you, or your product or service. These will probably be out of context and reflect more poorly on the reviewer rather than on you.

However, you have to start somewhere. The good reviews will far outweigh the bad reviews. And think about this.

Oprah Winfrey wasn't 'THE' Oprah Winfrey' when she first started out. We know who she is because she persevered. We know who all the greats are because they persevered.

People make mistakes in business all the time. It's only a tragedy if we don't learn from the mistakes.

How to feel safe and persevere

A 'rite of passage' is a ceremony or event marking an

important stage in someone's life, especially birth, the transition from childhood to adulthood or marriage.

We have created a 'rite of passage' page on the website www.abundance-magic.co.uk/peackock

I'm looking forward to hearing about your first disaster on your road to riches. If/when it happens, please take a moment and write it down now on our website. The 'abundance magic' group are all here to cheer you on.

We have all fallen out of a tree at one time or another, picked ourselves up, shared the story with the group and got back on that branch!

You can too. We are rooting for you. We want you to succeed. I am personally your biggest fan!

I have written down some of the really bad things I did in my early days as an example too. Write them down and release them.

Write down your fears:
www.abundance-magic.co.uk/brave
Then celebrate releasing them. If you need any inspiration ...you can read some of my whoppers on that page too.

You don't have to be famous to write a book or set up a course. You don't need to be perfect. You will become perfect through the experience of creating. The journey will help you hone your skills.

What qualifies me to write this book and produce these cards?

I started and stopped writing many times as all the fears and doubts crept into my mind. But I was determined to add to the world's conversation on the subject of creating abundance. I chased away the negative thoughts about being inferior or not qualified and started writing. I knew I was onto something when the book literally flowed out of my mind and into reality.

Your opinion matters and there is a reason why you feel motivated to write down your own thoughts about a specific subject. You won't know until you try.

There is a reason why you feel motivated to create something and share it with the world. Tap into that energy and start right now!

MONEY INSIGHTS:

1. What could you do to create a passive income?
2. Add to the conversation, the world is waiting to hear from you
3. Write down and release your fears

DOG

Loyalty, protection, love.

The universe has your back!

5

DOG

Man's best friend is known for its loyalty and the fact that it will do anything that you train it to do, because ultimately it wants to please you.

Your subconscious or the universe is exactly like a dog's loyalty. It will do anything you ask it to do. You have to, however, give it clear, easy to understand tasks.

If you asked your pet dog to go fetch you some 'happiness' or some 'wealth', or 'more time with your family and friends'. It would look at you confused and actually feel hurt and uncomfortable that it cannot deliver these things to you.

Pulling this card is a strong message from your subconscious mind that it needs clearer goals from you.

Example:

When I first started my branding business I was working

for peanuts. I soon realised this wasn't a sustainable business model. I attracted lots of clients, who didn't really appreciate the work I was doing, they were attracted by the price in the first instance.

I needed to put my prices up. I also first needed to work out what I wanted more of. I knew that I didn't want more 'cheap' clients.

I had very poor goals in those days. I hadn't bothered to write them down and I hadn't defined them clearly.

The old goal was something like:

I want to do some graphic design work for some people who will pay me.

I hope that the universe will send me clients to match my talents. I won't tell the universe what these exact talents are. I hope the universe can guess what I truly want to achieve deep down on a soul level.

I won't write down my goals or anything like that, I will just expect the universe to guess what I am good at and just like know that I will like do a good job when I get the clients.'

If your goal is anything like that, then good luck creating wealth and abundance!

You really do need to define your goals in order to get the right customers.

I spent some time reflecting on what I am truly good at… by focusing on 'logo design' (something I love and am really good at) I was able to attract entrepreneurs who need logos for their new businesses.

It is really important that you clearly define your goals in great detail.

My new goal was something like this:

I want to attract positive, energetic clients who are starting a new business, who need a new logo and who are as passionate about their brand as I am.

I want to work with clients who can afford to pay me what I am worth. Clients who appreciate my work and who are aligned with my ethos of 'sustainable growth'.

I want to work with clients who love my style of design, who will place all their orders for marketing materials with me and who will refer me on to their peers.

They don't need to be local, provided they can work with technology, the entire process can be done online or via email.

I'm so pleased to report that once I had defined these goals and written them out and put them in a prominent place so that my subconscious mind could see them clearly and regularly, as well as feel the energy around them, things changed for the better.

My 'faithful hound' or my 'subconscious brain' was able

to go out into the world and 'sniff out' the right clients and track them down for me.

Writing this type of goal down meant that every time I went out networking, the tone of voice I used when explaining 'who we are' and 'what we offer' changed because of the underlying goal which was the foundation to my sales and marketing efforts.

I was channelling the energy of the dog every time I went out networking. When I designed any new page on the website, I invoked the dog animal spirit to help guide me to achieve my goals. To stay focused, loyal and faithful to my goals. And 'fetch' the much needed clients to the business.

There were one or two oddities that appeared straight away, a test from the universe to make sure I stuck to my goal. I politely declined working with the 'cheap' clients, referred them on to other designers who I knew would be a good fit for them.

By staying 'faithful' to my goals, I am pleased to say I now attract my 'ideal clients' all the time.

It's important that you are ready emotionally and mentally for the odd 'wrong' customer to appear. This is very normal and great practice for you to say 'no' to them. It reinforces who you are and what you are about and is a fantastic stepping stone to where you want to be.

If you need more help in this area and want to learn

more about being true and faithful to yourself and your goals, then read Chapter 11 'TRUTH' and follow the exercises outlined at the end of that chapter.

MONEY INSIGHTS:

1. Make sure your goal is tangible
2. Create a visual icon or symbol of that goal
3. Stay faithful to your goals

SQUIRREL

Thrifty, smart, savings.

I'm sorry, I forgive you, I love you, I have moved on!

11

SQUIRREL

Be prepared and stay focused on your goals.

Squirrels are well known for gathering their food during the summer months and storing them ahead of the long, lean winter months.

If you have picked this card, think about your saving habits. Are you able to save money and store up some reserves?

If you have money blocks around saving and have to spend money the minute you earn it, you may need to do some work on this subject.

I remember my mum complaining endlessly about the fact that money came in one hand and went out the other... guess what? I picked up this negative trait around money and always spent every penny I earned until I got in control of this habit and healed this specific money block.

PHYSICAL SOLUTION

The practical, physical way to reach a goal is really simple:

- Write down the problem... (Example: *I spend every cent. I am unable to save any money*)
- Write down who caused the problem (Example: My mum constantly complained that money came in one hand and went out the other. I picked up the habit too, so I have to forgive myself too)
- Tell these people you forgive them, or if it's too embarrassing then just forgive them out loud when you are alone. Saying the words out loud cements them in your subconscious mind and helps it understand that the path ahead includes forgiveness.

There should be no shame or guilt attached to this money block in the future. It was done, and it is over now. We have forgiven everyone involved. It is no longer an issue.

Here is a good mantra to say out loud as a pattern interrupter when you feel the urge to spend your last penny:

I'm sorry, I forgive you, I love you, I have moved on.

I had to forgive my parents (energetically and verbally) for passing this (and other) poor money traits on to me. I forgave myself for years of spending. I allowed myself to start a savings account and after some time, I could

149

enjoy looking at the money in my savings account. Another great way to create abundance is by creating different saving accounts for different areas in your life.

Each savings account should have a different name. One for treats and holidays, one for home improvements, one for charity and one for the unexpected expenses that can manifest in our lives.

METAPHYSICAL SOLUTION

If you have experienced the benefit of meditation in the past, then you may want to try the meditation I have developed to forgive yourself and others on a very deep level.
www.abundance-magic.co.uk/forgiveness

In conclusion, be smart, plan your finances. Squirrel away some money each month so that you have a buffer to take care of emergencies. Identifying your money blocks and remove them by forgiving where necessary.

MONEY INSIGHTS:

1. STOP all negative talk around money
2. Forgive yourself and others for poor money habits and traits
3. Set up saving pots. Even if it's £5 per month
4. Review your saving pots, often

BEARS

Strength, family, vitality, courage, health, strong willed.

Who do you think you are?

7

BEARS

A fierce grizzly bear is a force to be reckoned with. If you pulled this card this week, you may need to channel your inner grizzly bear.

No need to be nasty or aggressive, but harness the energy of the bear animal spirit, this will help you to be strong when focusing on what's important.

Bears symbolize introspection and intuition blended with instinct. This book is written with the sensitive, spiritual person in mind, who can, let's face it, be a bit of a pushover sometimes.

When I started my branding business I would intuitively come up with a price that I knew that particular customer could afford.

Having empathic tendencies meant that I would know instinctively if my prices were too high for that person's budget. This was a huge mistake to make as I basically gave hours of my time away to people who didn't always appreciate it.

Instead, you should instinctively set up your prices based on your own intuition of what you need and what you are worth.

Do not make up prices to suit the individual client. 'Set your stand out' as you are, tell the world who you are and then the right clients will be attracted to you.

When I first started my business, I was the perfect pushover. I was the softest, cuddliest bear in the world. Think of Baloo from the Jungle Book. On the subject of money, I didn't want to think about it at all. I wanted to *'Forget about my worries and my strife'*

Example:
One client came to me, hat in hand and said all the key words a fledgling business owner says... 'We don't have much money in the business yet'... etc. etc., I fell for the pitch and submitted an incredibly low quote... Only to find out weeks later that this business person was a multi-millionaire and could easily afford a lot more than the pittance I charged for their design work.

This card may be a nudge to you to put your prices up, review how you are conducting your business. Channel your inner grisly bear. You will be so glad you did.

If you are bartering work instead of charging real money, promise yourself you will stop that immediately and start charging actual money. You cannot pay a mortgage, your rent, your salary, or even staff wages with bartering. I know it's tempting but it's worth paying people for their services and expect the same in return.

Your subconscious will take a backseat, put it's feet up and arrange a nice long hibernation if it thinks you are not serious about making money. Put your mind to work and prove to the universe you are a serious player.

Bears, like squirrels, are able to store up reserves for the long harsh winter. Make sure you have a plan in place to save money. (See squirrel chapter) Perhaps you have a tax bill coming up or you have new equipment that you need to purchase.

Putting some money away each month will help you plan and it also tells your subconscious mind that you are serious about money and you deserve to earn more. It may feel a bit scary at first, but in no time at all, you won't even miss that small amount of money and it really is a game-changer.

Who the hell do you think you are?
What makes you so special?

Did you hear words like this in your formative years?

I did, and once again, my sensitive side took all of this to heart and I felt smaller than small when I heard these words. It took me years and years to feel comfortable with who I actually am.
If you ever hear these words (or similar) in the back of your mind, asking you the question of 'who do you think

you are', 'what makes you so special' 'why should you run your own business' or 'who are you to write a book'. Channel your inner bear to fight off the negativity and challenge this feeling.

Remember also, to forgive anyone who hasn't taken you seriously. This may even be yourself.

There is a lovely forgiveness meditation on the website if you would like to forgive at a deeper level: www.abundance-magic.co.uk/forgiveness

One last thought from bear is to be brave. We have so many fears around so many things, am I good enough, thin enough, attractive enough to be wealthy?

Some of us may even may be afraid of having too much money.

This is not surprising when you think of how many children's stories and films depict the evil villain as the wealthy but misguided character who preys upon poor wretched souls.

I'm not sure about you, but I was raised on fairy tales and bedtime stories that warned me time and again that wealthy wasn't always good!

Hollywood films are all over this concept too. Think of all the wealthy evil characters in modern day films and television. We are bombarded constantly with images and tales of infamous characters who do their best to take over the world and who take advantage of anyone who cannot stand up to them. Poor Cinderella is left to clean up after everyone else has gone to the ball.

If you then translate this into your daily life and money goals, you may be self-sabotaging in order to prevent yourself from becoming wealthy (evil).

PHYSICAL SOLUTION

If we think about this logically, the fact that you are worried about it in the first place means that you are unlikely to become the 'miserly Scrooge' or the 'evil queen' that you read about. You are far more likely to do good with your money and 'save' more people than you can possibly imagine.

If you need a fairytale character to believe in, just think of 'Prince Charming'. He is the wealthy, kind, brave champion who continually chooses the path of good despite his wealth and family connections. Prince charming supports charities and is always determined to fight evil and win the day.

One of my favourite modern day super hero's is Oprah Winfrey. I always feel inspired when I think of her amazing journey and the wonderful people she has helped along the way. There are many to choose from if you take some time, think about your modern day hero and see if you can relate to them and attune your wealth goals to theirs.

I personally believe that you will be good or evil despite your bank balance.

A practical step you can take right now to help ease your mind from the fears of having too much wealth and 'power', is to write a list of which charities you will support when you have hit your first, second and third financial targets.

If your subconscious mind sees your fabulous goal to support a charity or set up foundation, it will be super motivated to help you achieve your goal in the first place. And just ask yourself...who better to decide which charities should receive financial aid than your good self?

Why shouldn't you be in charge of saving the world? Improving the lives of people or animals who need help? Think of all the good you can do with your wealth!

METAPHYSICAL SOLUTION

I mentioned being brave throughout this chapter. It can be incredibly difficult to feel brave when you are feeling nervous about an upcoming event, you are surrounded by negativity or if things aren't going your way and you can literally feel yourself spiralling downwards. I felt this way recently (despite my recent successes and physical evidence that 'I'm on the right path') it can happen anywhere, anytime.

I had been invited to speak at an event where I knew there would be press, photographs, video recordings, the Mayor was due to be there too and I felt panic rise up inside of me every time I thought about my speech.

Some of the speech was going to be 'ad libbing', based on the speakers who would be speaking just before me. I gave myself a moment to identify the problem and it came to me: I am getting better and better at prepared speeches but 'off the cuff' is still so nerve racking.

I tried logical reasoning to conquer my fears first but it wasn't working. I could feel the crippling, familiar, white hot fear and panic rise up inside me each time I imagined myself delivering my speech. I can normally visualise myself coming off the stage, the crowd is applauding my performance and everything went well. This time, it wasn't working, I kept imagining the worst.

I was in the throws of a downward tornado spiral, full throttle, hurtling toward disaster. Hurricane FEAR was taking over and she was taking no prisoners!

I even started to come up with a hundred excuses as to why I wouldn't be able to attend the event in the first place. Something was wrong. And I had to do something fast to prevent the inevitable downward spiral.

I decided to bring some high vibrational energy into play.

By channelling my inner grizzly bear I faced the problem head on... The 'AXIS PRACTICE' from chapter 5, 'ACKNOWLEDGEMENT' became an hourly event.

By breathing deeply and channelling the energy from mother earth and my higher self, I was able to remove these annoying fears and stay grounded.

Being grounded meant that I was able to keep my attention on my goals and stay focused on the bigger picture of what needed to happen in order to achieve them.

Once I was grounded I was then able to visualise the positive end result.

Guess what, I had a standing ovation at the end of the speech and people were still talking about it a week later... RESULT!

MONEY INSIGHTS:

1. Take a hard look at your profit margins and how you do business. If necessary put your prices up
2. Trust your intuition
3. Set up savings accounts or top them up if they are already set up
4. Be brave. Feel the fear and challenge the fear

PEACOCK

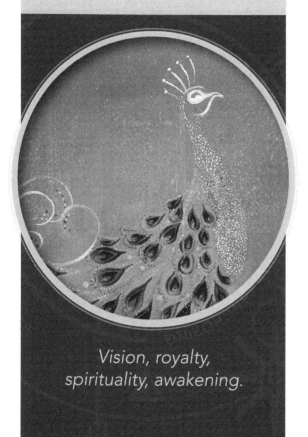

*Vision, royalty,
spirituality, awakening.*

As proud as a peacock!

8

PEACOCK

'Genius and virtue are to be more often found clothed in gray than in peacock bright.'
Van Wyck Brooks

Some people in this world are arrogant and annoying, I doubt they are reading this book!

This book and these cards are more likely to be in the hands of a sensitive soul. Someone who actually could benefit from feeling some pride about who they are and what they have to offer the world.

I feel like pride was a trait that was knocked out of me as a child. The society I grew up in didn't want me to feel proud or boastful. Which is a good thing to a point.

But as a sensitive person, I took the lesson too far. If I won anything or did anything well, I would immediately squash any feelings of pride. If I felt anything remotely like the feeling of pride I would push the feeling right down inside me and make it as small as I could.

Getting the balance just right is so important. No one likes those arrogant annoying proud people who are boastful and self involved. But if you are sensitive you should take time to feel pride. Allow this emotion a place in your heart and your head.

Think of the lives you have touched. The world is a better place because you exist.

This is such an important card. If you have drawn this card it's a sign that you need to acknowledge your progress so far.

I don't care how small the win. Even if it's just the starting point of things to come, if you have only just put down the name of your new business. That is a huge win and I would appreciate it if you acknowledged it. So will your subconscious and your future wealthy self.

There are many ways to acknowledge and anchor in positive achievements. If you have someone to share these with, do so now!

If you don't have anyone in your world who would understand, then share with us. We have all been there and know what it feels like when people around you don't quite 'get' you. They may be perfectly lovely people but their world is a little different to ours.

Log on to our proud as a peacock page:

www.abundance-magic.co.uk/peacock
and tell us what achievements you have had this week, this month or this year.

Tell us anything at all.

This action may seem cheesy or weird at first but guess what... it's helping your subconscious mind to understand where it needs to go and what it needs to do to help you achieve your goals.

Our peacock page is a safe place where everyone is welcome to tell us how they are doing, let us know what happened to make you feel happy.

Did you win a new client?
Finish a chapter in your book?
Earn a bit more money this month? ...Or even save some money?

Anchor in this positive step toward your goals by writing it down and telling the world. I personally cannot wait to hear from you no matter how small the win.

Example: One of my favourite things in the world is free coffee, if I get a free coffee I feel like the cat that got the cream. It's a small thing but it makes my day!

MONEY INSIGHTS:

1. It's a good thing to feel proud of yourself
2. Forgive anyone who didn't acknowledge your achievements (even if that's you)

3. Write down your achievements in a journal, or in the sand or on our page, www.abundance-magic.co.uk/peacock

OSTRICH

Wealth, abundance, fertility.

What are you hiding from?

9

OSTRICH

I grew up in sunny South Africa. Surrounded by a myriad of birds, animals and insects. One of my favourite stories I heard when I was young is about the ostrich. It's such a large bird and it has the strangest habit of hiding its head behind something if it feels afraid.

The ostrich believes that if it can't see the problem, then the problem can't see it.

The hilarious truth is that its body is gigantic and can easily be seen. Whilst the ostrich's small head can be hidden behind a rock or mound of sand and the rest of it's huge body sticks out very obviously.

These birds stand around 2.7m tall and can weigh as much as 159kg – that's around 1m taller than the average man, and the weight of two men combined!

Not only that, the ostrich might not be able to fly, but boy can it run! Using it's long legs, powerful thighs and strong feet, this big bird can cover five metres in a single stride and reach speeds of over 70km per hour!

If an ostrich is cornered by a hungry predator, such as a lion, cheetah, leopard or hyena. It will kick with a force powerful enough to kill. Each two-toed foot is armed with a ten centimetre sharp claw. So predators had better beware!

If you pulled this card you may need to think about what you are hiding from?

I used to put my 'head in the sand' whenever the money subject came up. I was terrified of money (what me? handle the finances... are you kidding?)

It's true, I would do just about anything to not have to deal with money. But guess what? If you want to build and grow a business, if you want to have any kind of sensible wealth and if you want a business you can be proud of, you have to face your money fears head on!

Don't try to hide behind a rock when you actually have everything you need to be successful.

You need to know how much money is coming in, how much is going out. When to put your prices up and you need to be able to confidently send out quotes to customers.

Plan ahead for your VAT, Corporation tax and ensure you have enough money to purchase new equipment, pay wages etc.

Money is at the heart of all good businesses. Make sure you take care of that heart. Make sure you feed it the right amount of money, exercise it daily by checking your bank balance.

That's all well and good you say, but perhaps you feel the way I used to feel and how do you get from there to here?

It's really important that you start to get excited about money. I know... I know... it's easier said than done. However, if I can do it, so can you.

I have activated the magic money miracle within myself and I would love for you to join me too. Harness the power of your inner ostrich, stand tall and proud and exercise those strong legs and sharp claws. Take strong determined strides toward your own magic money miracles.

Here are some amazing tips to get you started:

STEP ONE

One of the most important parts of running a successful business is sending out quotes in the first place. I had a huge block around this and desperately hated sending out quotes. The way I got around this was twofold:

1. For my regular clients I used my online quoting software system, I could easily login, review what I had charged the client previously and fairly painlessly adjust

the new invoice depending on what they were asking for. This quick system freed up hours of time.

The software allows you to check what clients owe you and what they paid for the service last time. If you have any discounts in place then you can add them confidently to any new invoices.

2. The second type of quote is for new clients. I developed a lovely document filled with examples of our work and putting all my work into this format (creative and visual) made me feel proud to send out a quote.

It also helped me to put my prices up when I needed to. By showing off the wonderful case studies and examples of designs I had created for other business, I lifted my energy up in this area, activating the light magic energy made me feel deserving of the money I was charging.

By no means was I expensive but to some people I was a bit pricey. Whenever I feel the fear building up inside me about being too expensive for some people, I remind myself: 'you get what you pay for'.

I always go above and beyond for my clients, I supply unlimited revisions on most projects and always make sure my customers look good in front of their customers... So of course I must charge for the value I bring to my client.

STEP 2

I insist on a 50% deposit or clients can pay over 12 months if they sign a contract. This weeds out the time wasters and helps me focus on working for clients who are as serious about their branding and marketing as I am.

STEP 3

Fake it till you make it! I taught myself to say things in emails and on the phone that I didn't quite believe yet.

I write the sunniest emails to clients. It didn't take too long before I started to feel the sunshine energy around sending quotes and invoices.

And guess what, the universe and my clients responded accordingly. If you respect yourself and your money and your time, the universe will too!

STEP 4:

Start counting how much money you are receiving. When my husband joined the business he asked me how much money I was earning. I couldn't answer. I had no idea what I was earning until I started to count each penny that came into the business.

Sure I was doing all the reconciling and preparing files for the accountant to prepare the VAT files every quarter, but I had no idea how much money was coming in every day, week or month.

In order to get in control of this subject, I started to add everything up on a piece of paper, every day. Every time I had a some money came into the bank account I added it up on a separate piece of paper.

At first, the idea of counting every penny, made me think of the well known 'Scrooge' fairytale character. I had a negative association with his personality. I just couldn't see myself spending my days stacking up coins on a desk and counting them every five minutes to make sure they were still there. It made me feel miserly and mean.

The energy around this idea for me was thick dark, gooey, stuck energy. Think of stinking swamp water... 'Yuck'...
No wonder I didn't know how much money was coming into the business on a daily basis. I had huge money blocks around the idea.

So what could I do?

I had to face my fears and stop hiding behind the excuse that I might look like a 'Scrooge' if I count my money every day.

I also decided that because I was going to throw everything at my money problem and because I had nothing to lose I would give it a go.

I started counting everything.

I love it so much now that I cannot wait to include

even the smallest penny found in the street. It became a game. My subconscious mind loves games. In no time at all I was finding money everywhere, I felt light, abundant and, for the first time, happy about the subject of money.

I sincerely hope you will join me in counting your pennies, lifting your money blocks and activating your money miracles.

Download our free App:

'Money INSIGHTS'
and start seeing the benefits today.

MONEY INSIGHTS:

1. Check your bank balance every day
2. Send out invoices punctually
3. Send out beautiful quotes that spark joy
4. Send out statements if necessary to chase money and improve your cash flow
5. Set up VAT and Corporation tax savings accounts in the business bank account
6. Download the App: Money INSIGHTS and start adding it all up

CHEETAH

Self – esteem,
speed, focus.

Carp Diem, Seize the day!

10

CHEETAH

Cheetahs are designed for speed. They prefer to prey on smaller wild animals as they don't have the weight of a lioness to help them pull down larger animals but they have speed and agility on their side.

I was lucky enough to visit the wild cheetah project in South Africa. The interesting thing about visiting this endangered species in their enclosure was that the game ranger hand fed the cheetah female and allowed one of our group to get off the Land Rover and take photos of the cheetah. Up close and personal!

Our companion was standing about a meter away from the cheetah, happily snapping away and the Cheetah was the picture of peace and tranquillity. She gently and slowly walked up to the game ranger and sat down and waited for him to hand her her lunch. She gently sank her teeth into the carcass and waited for him to let go before she moved any further (the picture of domestic docility). If there were any male cheetahs nearby I did not see them.

This was quite an experience for all of us and also quite different from our next visit which was to the wild dog project in an enclosure not far from these graceful, wild cats.

When we got to the wild dog enclosure the game ranger stayed on the Land Rover the entire time, he insisted we did too (not that any of us needed convincing). And he threw the lunch to the wild dogs who were growling and snarling and barking and making a right fuss. They tore into their lunch and fought each other for the best bits.

Speed is everything when winning more business. 9 times out of 10 a client will go with the first person who shows up. This might mean the first person to reply to a social media request, send a quote, make a phone call or send an enticing email.

I personally have won new clients because I was the first one on the scene.

Naysayers have warned me on more than one occasion, that if you answer a request for a quote too quickly it looks like you don't have enough business because you are not good at your business and therefore not busy.

What nonsense!!

If you run your business properly, you should have enough time in each day to send out a quote or make a call or even send a graceful email saying you will be in touch with a proposal as soon as possible.

Obviously there have been times when I physically could not answer the request for a quote that instant or even that same day. In these cases, get into the habit of sending a holding email or social media response saying something like:

'Dear... This sounds like an amazing project which I would love to be a part of, thank you for the opportunity to quote, I will have the fee proposal with you by...
- Lunch time tomorrow
- Thursday morning latest
- By the end of the week.

Using this holding communication systems, means that existing clients and potentially new clients feel respected and are more than happy to wait for the quote to come through.

They totally get that I may be working on another project and yet, I have taken a moment to acknowledge them and their needs.

I also back up all my fee proposals with excellent examples of my work. Links to my website and testimonials from happy clients.

With regards to speed and the 'bigger picture', in her book 'Big Magic' Elizabeth Gilbert reminds us that great opportunities don't hang around for forever.

If you have an inspired idea, act on it quickly.

After reading her book I ramped up my efforts to get my own book finished.

If you are not careful, someone else will have the same inspired idea and might get there before you do.

Get your priorities right, hang your party hat up whilst you get your valuable thoughts down on paper and out into the world.

MONEY INSIGHTS:

1. Reply quickly to potential work opportunities.
2. Get your thoughts down on paper and into the world as fast as possible.
3. Respect yourself and your clients and potential clients and they will respect you back.

FISH

Fertility, creativity, good luck, transformation, health, serenity, intelligence, happiness and endurance.

NEVER stop questioning!

11

FISH

The mesmerizing gold fish, take all who gaze upon it into journeys of deeper perceptive states.

By increasing your perception, you improve your energy and allow more wealth and prosperity to flow into your life.

We have a lot of Pisces people in our family. I have definitely learned a lot from these wise souls. I am grateful to have known and shared living space with so many of them. They seem to have 'seen it all' and 'done it all' before. They tend to be emotionally intelligent and have a patience about them that I can only marvel at and envy.

They are incredibly good with money too.

As with most Chinese symbols, the carp has a legend attached to it. According to legend, the carp is noted for its strength and bravery because it swims against the current, upwards, 'mastering' falls and ending up at a gate on the Yellow River called Dragon Gate. The carp turns into the revered Celestial Dragon when it makes a final leap over the last rapids.

If you have drawn this card, you should consider trying creative ways to solve your business and money problems.

If you have been putting off a project for a while, you could harness the energy of these revered fish and think about swimming in a different direction, or leaping up out of the water.

Stop trying so hard to fit in when you were born to stand out. By swimming in a different direction to everyone else, you may solve your problem.

If you feel like you have creativity blocks from time to time and they prevent you from achieving your goals, now is the time to focus on clearing the blocks.

I read all of Edward De Bono's books in my early twenties and they were life changing. I seldom have a creative block because of all the training I did and conceptual thought processing invoked from these readings.

The term 'PO' was created by Edward de Bono as part of a lateral thinking technique to suggest forward movement, that is, making a statement and seeing where it leads to.

It is an extraction from words such as hypothesis, suppose, possible and poetry, all of which indicate forward movement and contain the syllable "po."

For example, Sales are dropping off because our product is perceived as old fashioned.

po: Change the colour of the packaging
po: Call it retro
po: Sell it to old people
po: Sell it to young people as a gift for old people
po: Open a museum dedicated to it
po: Market it as a new product

Some of the above ideas may be impractical, not sensible, not business-minded, not politically correct, or just plain daft. The value of these ideas is that they move thinking from a place where it is entrenched to a place where it can move.

References
Edward de Bono. The Mechanism of Mind (1969). ISBN 0-224-61709-5, introduced the term po in chapter 34, The New Functional Word
Edward de Bono. Po: A Device for Successful Thinking (1972). ISBN 0-671-21338-5
Edward de Bono. Po: Beyond Yes and No (1973). ISBN 0-14-021715-0

Edward de Bono. Serious Creativity (1992). ISBN 0-00-255143-

My point is, that by looking at the problem from a different angle you can often solve the problem.

If you get out of your fish bowl, you may have a different perspective.

I am a huge fan of 'ask the audience' too. If you are really getting nowhere fast, then ask a friend or family member (that you trust) what they would do.

You can also ask your brain a question the way Einstein did:

To really think creatively, our brain needs to be fed quality questions. The story goes that Albert Einstein's mum used to ask him everyday: What good question did you ask today?

Instead of asking 'how was your day' she would give his brain a quality question to ponder.

What you ask is crucial for your business and your life.

When you ask your brain, it will give you an answer and whether your answer will be good or not often depends on your question.

If I ask, what is 1+1 there is only one answer, however if I ask what is ?+?=2 the possibilities are endless: 0.25 + 1.75 and 0.5 + 1.5 and so fourth. (Reference: https://www.loromedia.com/how-to-think-creatively/)

MONEY INSIGHTS:
1. There is no such thing as a creative block
2. Change your perspective. Try super-size problems, or down size them, turn them upside down or inside out
3. Ask the right question. Spend a few minutes rephrasing your question and give it to your brain to find the solution

ELEPHANT

*Power, strength,
tenderness.*

Learn to delegate.

12

ELEPHANT

"If you want to do a few small things right, do them yourself. If you want to do great things and make a big impact, learn to delegate."
John C. Maxwell

This ever gentle and wise giant exemplifies focused power and strength.

If you have been feeling slow and perhaps even a little unproductive lately, take heart, the universe is on your side and wants you to trust that no matter what, you are perfect. You have all the magical gifts you need to be a star, to achieve your dreams, take care of yourself and your loved ones.

Avoid bouncing around from subject to subject right now and focus rather on achieving one big important goal. Create a magical powerhouse goal that makes you feel strong and energetically abundant.

Before you start each day close your eyes and ask your higher self what is really important to work on right now.

What will enhance your creative magical inner being and aid the work of your higher purpose.

In the wild, a mother elephant has help with the babies from other elephants – who are known as 'Aunties'. A new mother will choose her aunties and together they will raise the baby.

Are you trying to do too much yourself?

If you have pulled this card this week, it's a sign that you could be doing too much yourself. If you have a mammoth goal to reach it may be more than worth your while to employ people or use software or systems to help achieve your goals.

You need to have time to work on your business as well as in it. Think about automating some of your systems and administrative tasks.

Also consider employing a freelancer to help with some of the work load. You may not have the spare capital to employ another full time member of staff so start with a freelancer.

It's also worth writing up your systems and processes for your business, this will help your employees, to understand their job, your company ethos and makes a better working experience for staff and clients.

In my business I use accounting software to help me with the day to day invoicing, quoting and reconciling of money. It costs a small fee every month but it is well worth it compared to the hours I used to have to spend amalgamating everything. My accountant can log in to the dashboard and prepare VAT and I have access to all the figures for the business, day or night. Result!

I have also built up relationships with tried and trusted suppliers to help me achieve my goals. Too often entrepreneurs think that they have to do it all themselves. This is simply not true. It does take time to build up relationships and set up systems but well worth the effort.

I also find that if I can't move forward on a project for some reason (usually it's because I am an empath and pick up other peoples stuck energy) if I get someone else involved, their energy changes the 'stuckness' in me because invariably they ask questions and these questions shake me out of the client's energy and into energetic action.

It sounds weird but I urge you to try it.

MONEY INSIGHTS:

1. Create a magical powerhouse goal that makes you feel strong and energetically abundant
2. It's okay to ask for help
3. Get the right kind of help, it may be software or it may be a person

HONEY BEE

*Community, brightness
and personal power.*

Better together!

13

HONEYBEE

Where would we humans be without the fabulous
energy of the honey bee?

Einstein believed so deeply in the importance of Bees
to the ecosystem that he predicted if Bees disappeared
humans would not survive more than four years
afterward.

When this card shows up, it is a sign that you are ready
for change.

When you start to live the life you were meant to, and
lean into the wave of new experiences, your business
and personal life may start to look quite different to the
way it does right now.

When you start focusing on your goals to the degree
that they start to actualise, your friends and family might
feel you are changing in a way that doesn't suit them.
This is to be expected and you can prepare yourself by

being ready for the lashing out or tricky conversations you have with them.

However, it's important that you keep your eyes on your goals. This is your life. You shouldn't try to live the life they have ear marked for you. If you do, you will be unhappy, unfulfilled and you wont be able to achieve the abundance that you are dreaming of.

You may lose friends along the way. They may not like the fact that you disappear on them. Drink less, get more sleep, less partying and more work. However, you need to be serious about your goals and do what it takes to actualise them.

Finding your tribe. Your tribe can change as your journey changes. I remember being in my twenties and feeling the deep sadness that comes with the loss of a tribe. The people I shared my earlier education with are no longer a part of my life, and haven't been for years. I do miss the idea of them, however, I felt I out grew that scene and wanted to focus on my career.

I did get a bit of flack from that. I remember thinking though, if they don't want what's best for me, then they can't really be good friends. Now can they?

I have spent some time forgiving them. It took me a while but eventually I was able to do the work necessary to forgive their actions against me.

'True friends will meet again after moments or life times'.
- Richard Bach

I will always be friends with the more advanced souls that I have met along the way, the ones who recognise that it is not always practical to remain great friends or BFF's when life and goals and careers and family get in the way.

We hold no grudges, when one or the other goes off to complete another part of their life's journey and if I bumped into them somewhere, sometime, we would pick up right where we left off. These are true friends. The kind I look forward to bumping into, the kind who lift my heart and spark joy in my life.

I have come to accept, however, that my tribe needs to change as I change. It makes sense. Us humans are all evolving at different levels and stages.

When you join the conversation, and take part in the evolution of the human species, you are being true to your nature and you should celebrate that fact.

I talk about tribes a lot in this chapter because I think it is important to find people who you can talk to, share stories with, the highs and the lows, because you shouldn't feel like you need to change the world on your own.

As your business takes of and you become the busy honey bee, you may find collaboration and working as a team, helping others and being helped is essential to your victory.

'Better together'. Anyone of us can be great on our own,

but we are all better when we act as part of a group or collaboration.

In my branding business, I meet entrepreneurs all the time, who are starting new products and services.

It would seem that they are all brilliant at something, and they can do a lot of the brand building themselves, however, they often ask me a host of questions that are probably outside of the scope of the brand building exercise and I realised this is because when you start a new business or launch a new product or service, you are often on your own a lot of the time. You need a sounding board to help you make decisions.

I started the online mastermind group for entrepreneurs to join who would like to grow their business and interact with others on the same wave length.

Other benefits:

- An Instant and Valuable Support Network
- Collaboration
- A Sense of Shared Endeavour
- Think Bigger
- Synergy
- New Perspectives
- Get Honest Feedback
- Advice
- Brainstorming

If you are part of a mastermind group already, that's great, but if you need to join some like minded

people then join us at
www.abundance-magic.co.uk/moneyinsights

MONEY INSIGHTS:

1. Be prepared to make new friends and allies when you start your new abundant life
2. Join a mastermind group

OWL

Wisdom, soul, intuition.

Trust your instincts!

14

OWL

Traditionally owls are a symbol of wisdom. They have fascinated humans throughout history, across all religions, continents and cultures.

Owls are connected with the wisdom of the soul or instinct, rather than intellectual wisdom.

Trust your instincts right now. It's good to share knowledge but make sure you are sharing with the right people.

This is the same for money. If friends and family approach you for money, it is wise to tread carefully.

Throughout time we have heard the many warnings about mixing family, friends and money. It can end horribly and you may lose touch with friends or loved ones forever over a misunderstanding around money... Ask yourself... Is it worth it?

Make sure that if you do lend money, it is with the crystal clear understanding that it will be paid back to you. If it is going to be paid back to you in instalments, insist that the first instalment happens straight away.

By insisting on the first instalment straight away, you send a clear message to the borrower that you are serious about money and you expect them to be too.

Also, make sure you write up a contract between yourself and the friend or family member to make sure they understand that you are serious about getting the money back.

This is actually for their own good. If they have poor money habits then the last thing you want to do is become an enabler. If you enable them to spend more money than they earn or can afford to pay back then you are ultimately adding to their financial downfall.

It would be far better if you could teach them how to make money or help them write a better CV. etc.

People with poor money habits tend to spend whatever they can get their hands on. If they won a million pounds in a few months time they would be stone broke again.

And it can happen to anyone.

Many celebrities go from being rich and famous to being involved in lawsuits or spending sprees that trigger bankruptcy.

One president was broke after leaving the Oval Office, and he had a famous author (who also went broke) write his memoirs.

MC Hammer, Meat Loaf, and 50 Cent all went from being top musicians with great wealth to bankruptcy and debt.

My parents used to give my brother a supermarket card with money on it, so that he could buy groceries when he was at University.

Of course, he could have bought beer from the store, but at least they knew they could top it up when he claimed he had ran out of funds and they could rest assured that he could purchase food if he needed to.

The important lesson here is what you do with the money when you earn it.

Do you have a great strategy for what to do with your money?

It is really tempting to go on a spending spree and take friends and family on all expenses paid holidays. Or buy outrageously expensive homes, cars, planes, yachts etc.

This sort of behaviour could ensure you end up straight back where you started. Or even worse, in debt!

Throughout this book, there are many wise suggestions on how to ensure you make money. This chapter deals with how you keep it once you have earned it.

I urge you to think of a long term financial strategy and invest wisely.

Property is a good investment. But make sure you are buying a property for the right reason. Buying the wrong property, just because you can, could be disastrous.

In 1989, actress Kim Basinger paid $20 million for a 1,691-acre town. Basinger was expected to create a tourist attraction such as a theme park or movie studio in Braselton, Georgia, but she instead declared bankruptcy and had to sell the property for a huge loss.

Whenever you purchase a property, make sure it's for the right reason. This is where your intuition comes into play once again. If the property feels right, you should get goosebumps when you think of it, it should fill your heart with joy.

If there is the slightest bit of doubt in your mind or heart, think twice. The property may not be for you.

To take this idea one step further, I have an interesting example of how the right property will show up at the right time, if you are patient and prepared to put a bit of effort into the investment. It is a big important investment after all, so shouldn't you give it the time and attention it deserves?

My husband (Ian) and I were looking for our next property to invest in. And we wrote down on paper what it should roughly include.

We painstakingly listed all the deal breakers and then all the practicalities that this long term investment should include.

We wanted something with long term prospects, that we could add our stamp to, and make some improvements too. I was searching online for properties that met our criteria, when something completely different caught my eye.

I shared it with Ian, and we both had the same reaction. We couldn't wait to go and see the property, put in an offer straight away and moved in 3 months later.

The property we bought was far superior in many ways to what we had on our list. It was much more 'us' and a bit less 'long term goal' but it was perfect for our needs and medium term goal. It would make the perfect stepping stone to our next property investment.

Looking back at our original thought process, I believe we were stretching too far into the future. We needed to think of a more immediate, medium term goal that could get us to our ultimate long term goal.

However, because we were so thorough with our plans and because we wrote everything down and weighed up all the pros and cons on each property, the universe was able to match what we were searching for with what we really needed. My subconscious brain was able to filter through all the elements we had written down and then make sure I was searching online at just the right moment.

It turns out that the property we bought, literally just went onto the market that week. If I hadn't opened my laptop to browse for a property that day, we would have missed it.

The actions we took, the planning meant that when the property was available we were ready to snap it up.

MONEY INSIGHTS:

1. Be careful when lending money.
2. When lending money, write up a contract and insist that the first instalment be paid straight away
3. Write down a solid, long term strategy
4. Write down a medium term strategy
5. Write down the little steps you can take to get you to your long term goal

DRAGONFLY

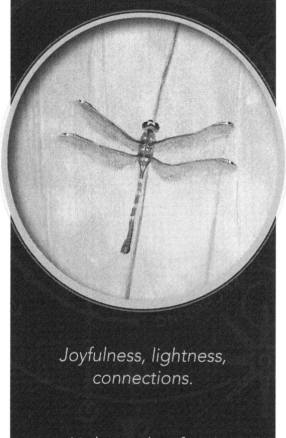

Joyfulness, lightness,
connections.

Little sparks of joy!

15

DRAGONFLY

Dragonflies travel at around 45 mph and can navigate in all directions, even backwards. It's known as a symbol of direction and purpose.

If you pulled this card then you may need some help with your mental agility. If you feel like you are up against a brick wall or fighting unseen obstacles, harness the dragonfly energy, zigzag your way through the obstacle, or look for another route, even if the route is longer, if you stay in motion, it will all be worth it and you could end up avoiding a nasty bump in the road of the short route.

It takes a lot more mindset than you think it will to become wealthy. Not everyone will make it. It takes dedication, focus and strength. But it is worth it, you are worth it.

One of the things I always say is that I eat for energy. If I do this then I find my mental agility is in top form. Feeling sluggish or mentally challenged, or experiencing any brain fog can be a result of your diet. Perhaps its time to review how you are treating your body. Do you consistently make sure you eat your 5 or more fruit and veg per day?

There is a well know saying: Health, Wealth and Happiness... and a jolly good reason why they start with the word 'Health'
If you don't have your health then what good is your wealth?

Think about little ways that you can improve your diet to give you the mental agility and physical energy to keep you focused on your goals.

I totally understand how tough it is to stay focused on goals when life takes up so much time. But we do live in an age when you can get your shopping delivered to you, you can be prepared and have quality fruit and vegetables available 24/7 to keep you healthy and on track.

I have been fascinated with dragonflies all my life, I have doodled them since I can remember. They always bring little sparks of joy whenever I see them.

Is there something in your past that sparks joy.

I'm reminded here of a rather successful chocolatier who decided to pack in her nine to five bank job and follow her dream. She had remembered the joy that chocolate sparked in her life. She wanted to create a vegan brand of chocolate to help others who share her milk allergy. Dissatisfied with the brands available in supermarkets, she set about creating her very own version.

If there is something you absolutely love to do and feel passionate about then it could be time to follow that dream.

Procrastination is something that is highlighted by the artful dragonfly. Dodge any procrastination now and find alternatives and habit interrupters to keep you focused on your goals.

Another reason why you may have pulled this card is that you may currently be caught up in the present, so much that you do not allow yourself any room for change and improvement.

The dragonfly is challenging you to break out and treat yourself to some new experiences. It's challenging you to broaden your horizons in such a way you can see what your current life really has to offer.

Is it time to sign up to a course or buy a book on a topic you could use toward manifesting your ultimate goal?

Look to the past, was there something you did well in the past that you could use now to help you obtain your future goals?

Is it time to join a new group?

If you are looking for like minded entrepreneurs who are interested in growing their businesses and raising their vibration around money. Then join our money mindset group:
www.abundance-magic.co.uk/moneyinsights

MONEY INSIGHTS:

1. Do something to enhance your mental agility
2. Look to the past to remind yourself what works well for you and harness this to help you achieve future goals
3. Shake things up, join a new group www.abundance-magic.co.uk/moneyinsights

CROCODILE

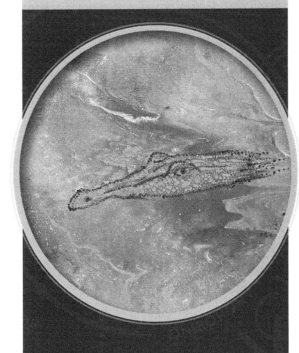

*Courage, strength, honour,
patience, speed, fear,
cunning, and primal power.*

What's your big idea?

16

CROCODILE

Crocodiles remind us that, in life, we cannot always be gentle and placid.

Children the world over are taught from a young age that its best to be gentle and sweet. 'Share your toys' they say, and behave sweetly. 'Its better to give than receive' etc.

I was a gentle, sensitive child, I took all these sayings to heart. However, I could have done with a few lessons on being forceful, or harnessing my inner strength and channelling some crocodile assertiveness. It would have helped me later in life in the work place. I was an incredibly shy teenager and painfully shy when I started work. When I look back now I cringe at how embarrassingly shy I was.

If you have pulled this card it might mean that you have a situation in your current work-life balance that needs a few teeth bared at it. You need to be fierce and confident. It's a jungle out there and you need to be ready to do what it takes to stay alive!

If someone is being a bully or taking you for granted, be brave and set them straight. There are lots of books about being assertive if you want a practical step by step approach to it and we have a meditation that will help you overcome your fears and stand in your power. www.abundance-magic.co.uk/fearless

Crocodile, reminds us to think of our primal instincts. This is also a good time to align with our inner child and make sure it is aligned to our higher nature. Read chapter 11 'TRUTH', for more insights.

If you have a 'big idea' to make money and/or a passive income, centre it around passing on your knowledge to the next generation.

Could you write a book and capture all your knowledge in a way that could help the next generation in your field?

Is there a course or system you could create that would share your knowledge to help the next generation and create wealth and abundance for you?

Watch out for procrastination when you pick this card. Put down that 'game boy' step away from the 'telly', keep distractions to a minimum.

Stop putting off until tomorrow what you can get done today!

MONEY INSIGHTS:

1. Channel your inner crocodile, face fears head on
2. Practice being assertive
3. How will your special talents help the next generation? Can you turn your knowledge into a course, a system or a book?

TURTLE

Ease, patience, wisdom, longevity.

Positivity breeds positivity and happiness is a choice!

17

TURTLE

Do you have what it takes to go the distance?

The western world depicts turtles as easygoing, patient, and wise creatures. Their long lifespan, slow movement, sturdiness, means they are symbolic of longevity.

Not everyone is suited to a life of serious wealth and abundance. Wealth creation requires long term dedication and commitment.

The one thing that the turtle card teaches us is that you need to surround yourself with positivity. The secret to long life and abundant success is positive thoughts and experiences.

It's so important to acknowledge good wins and positive outcomes, no matter how small.

My husband and I high five each other all the time for any positive outcome. From finding a parking outside a store to a lucky penny found on the floor, to winning a big new client contract.

Positivity breeds positivity and happiness is a choice.

Another way to stay positive is by taking responsibility for your beliefs because it gives you the power to change them.

No matter how tough your childhood was or how many times you were ill-treated, or told you were not worthy, that is no longer your reality, you can transform hate and resentment into love and empathy. Take ownership of your money mindset and create new positive habits around money.

I have a little mantra that I say when I am reminded about a negative money belief that was instilled in me as a child... You know the ones I mean, like:

'We can't afford that. Money doesn't grow on trees you know!'

As soon as I hear those word in the echoes of my mind, I say immediately: *'I have my own personal abundance river that flows abundantly and freely'*

I have another mantra which helps with fears of being wealthier than ones own parents:

My mantra: *'Everyone in my family loves me they want me to do well, they are cheering me on and they are inspired by my success.'*

Use the mantras or make up your own. You will then feel peaceful, happier, more productive and able to take action efficiently start your dream actions. That is true abundance!

MONEY INSIGHTS:

1. You are in it for the long haul
2. Find ways to surround yourself with positivity
3. Make sure you have some mantras at hand or pattern interrupters for times when you feel yourself slipping back into old habits
4. Forgiveness allows you to release past hurts and become rich
5. www.abundance-magic.co.uk/forgiveness

HORSE

*Power, strength,
freedom.*

You have hit the jackpot!

18

HORSE

WOW... Lucky you... You have hit the jackpot!

When horse comes galloping into your life energy.
Saddle up, you are in for the ride of your life. Hold on
tight and get your house in order.

Horse is an amazingly powerful animal. When Horse
energy represents your money goals, ambitions and
desires it is like winning the lotto!

If you have drawn this card, I'm extremely envious of
you right now. Drawing this card from the pack means
that there is more than enough motivation to carry you
through to achieve your financial goals.

When I say get your house in order. By this I mean,
make sure your fridge and freezer is well stocked.
Make sure you have nutritional meals planned and 'go
to' recipes that keep you healthy and satisfied, you
are going to need to focus on work right now so you

need to have your home and office in tip top working condition. Drink lots of water. Make sure you have access to good fresh filtered water to keep you going and energised.

You could also benefit right now from having your business 'house in order' Make sure you have systems and procedures in place to cope with the new workload and new customers coming in.

Horse is a creature of success and self-actualization.

When you know what drives you and put that awareness to work, you can go galloping into your future wealth and abundance faster than you ever thought possible.

If you have been planning to launch a new product or service. Do it now! Things are aligned for you. You should find just the right people, advertising or marketing opportunities. Doors are opening for you right now and its time to step on through.

I appreciate you might want to walk through the doors that are opening and if this is your first time launching a product or service then by all means walk gently through that door.But please do walk through it.

Don't miss this opportunity. Even if you are not completely polished or perfect, horse will lead you through and horse doesn't go through just any old door... the horse likes to go through fabulous, bright, shiny, hopeful doors. So if the doors open, trust your instincts obviously, but feel spurred on at this time.

If this is your second launch or you have been here before this is a time where you can make improvements to products or services. Run or gallop through the door and into new opportunities and profits. Harness this new found energy and make hay whilst the sun shines.

The last time I pulled the horse card, I remember the doors opening. I felt like I had to pinch myself. Was this really happening? I was introduced to just the right people at just the right time.

I remember before the pitch I was so nervous. I was meeting a rather large blue chip company. And I had to meet them at their offices, where I was sure the internet would fail on me and I was worried that I would end up fluffing the pitch for the new business.

I had about 3 days to prepare for the meeting and I had a heavy work load on that week over and above the stress of meeting a potentially huge client for the first time. This was an interesting conundrum and one that comes up all the time in business. How do you make sure you don't let your current clients down but also spend enough time preparing to win new business.

I spent at least half an hour meditating on how to prepare for the meeting in a way that could ensure I won the new business but that meant that I could work without the internet.

Eventually the idea came to me to dust off my trusty old physical portfolio... something I hadn't had to use for many years. I updated it, looked carefully at the pieces in there and then set my attention to creating a story around the pieces that would appeal to the potential new client.

IT WORKED! They loved my presentation. I won the business!

I was quite nervous (good nervous) and I knew I would be up against younger branding and design professionals, so I went 'old school', traditional and literally showed examples of my work that the potential client could touch and feel.

The horse card gave me the confidence to trust my intuition with my presentation. Incidentally, during the meeting, my internet dongle couldn't get a signal due to their thick office walls. And it was against their policy to give me a password to access their wifi so my instincts to go 'old school' were spot on.

Confidence is a huge part of winning new business.

When I first started my branding business, I was quiet, shy and felt I couldn't stand up for myself. I won new business purely by word of mouth referral. I did a good job and kept my prices sweet and pretty soon word spread that I did a good job at a good price and so the business grew.

I did have to have a lot of customers in order to make enough money to pay my bills at the end of the month.

I also struggled to put my prices up.

It felt like a huge leap of faith and I was sure I would lose customers. However, the next time I drew the horse card and I had been thinking of putting my prices up for a while, the card gave me the courage I needed to trust my intuition and, I took a deep breath and I did it.

And guess what. I lost a few customers but gained lots of new quality customers, who were prepared to pay me what I was worth and I therefore ended up working on projects I love and earned more money in the process. Result!

MONEY INSIGHTS:

1. It's time! Time to put your prices up. Time to market your service or product
2. Whether you walk or gallop, do it now!
3. Get your house in order, make sure you have a solid foundation to work from

FOX

*Discernment,
wisdom, cunning.*

*Accept the truth
and move swiftly on!*

19

FOX

Everything is so much clearer when you have the fox in your corner, helping you to achieve abundance.

Even if you are a gentle and kind soul, when you harness the energy of a fox, you will not hesitate to be crafty should the situation call for it.

Now is a time to be quick, act quickly and decisively to solve problems and move swiftly through challenges and obstacles. Trust your instincts.

You will be able to have a sixth sense around people's behaviours. You will know who to hire, who to fire. And how to get the best out of any situation.

I have never been sorry that I trusted my instincts. I have, however, been sorry when I have not trusted them.

Even if a situation looks good on paper, if your instincts say there is a problem around this person, product or business, then there will be.

It might be that the person, product or service is truly amazing in the eyes of the world at large... However, for whatever reason, they are just not right for you and your business right now.

Accept this truth and move swiftly on.

Now is not a time to spend wallowing or resting on your laurels, now is the time to get noticed. Launch a product or service. Hit the send button on an email campaign. Take the first step to something better. If you have had an idea to do something, learn something, launch something enter into a agreement with someone or something now is a great time.

If you cannot trust your instincts right now, if they feel clouded and you feel doubtful. Spend some time writing up a pros and cons list.

These are great tools to use when you cannot see the wood for the trees.

The fox energy will help you scan through the lists of pros and cons and land on a helpful solution.

In my late twenties, I was offered the choice of 3 jobs. I could not work out which one to take. I did the pros and cons list and they all ended up being pretty equal. I even looked at travel time to and from work, etc. I looked at salary, prospects everything, they were all 3 the same.

I then spent a small amount of time meditating on each one, and trusted my intuition in the end on which one to take.

The one that seemed to have the greatest prospects was not the one I took in the end. My instincts told me that there was something not quite right with the employer. I was interested to learn about six months later that the person who did take the job ended up as a scape goat and was fired, leaving the business with a nasty stigma attached to them.

Because I had inside knowledge of the role and responsibility awarded this person, I knew that they had not committed the crimes they were accused of.

It was also interesting that I even heard about this outcome because I seldom listened to the news and happened to have the radio on that day when the news was broad cast. I have never been so grateful in my life for trusting my instincts.

They are there for a reason. If you have picked this card it is a sign that you may need to sharpen your instincts and start trusting them again.

MONEY INSIGHTS:

1. Trust your instincts
2. Write up a 'pros' and 'cons' list
3. Don't dilly dally ... act now!

BUTTERFLY

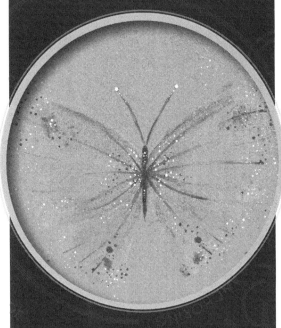

*Endurance, change,
hope, life.*

*You are a beautiful soul,
shine so that the whole world
can see your brightness!*

223

20

BUTTERFLY

Not only are butterflies beautiful to look at, they remind us of transformation and change. They are continually changing quite dramatically.

We learn about metamorphosis in our early child hood and the butterfly is an amazing example of this. First an egg then a worm then a larva and finally a beautiful butterfly.

Think about how you would like your business to evolve. Think about the shimmering sensation of light falling on a beautiful butterfly's wings, think about the hope and energetic charge that evokes in your mind.

NOW...

Write down your goals for your business.
What are you going to do, make, sell. What will spark joy in your life and the lives of others. Remember to write the goals with clarity. Read more in chapter 6

SYMBOLS

If you are already selling something think of how you can improve it, or what you need to do to energise your product or service...THEN put your written goal somewhere in your line of site, a place that you look at every day.

There is more about this in the chapter 8 entitled VISUALISATION

Some use the bathroom mirror, a great use of time in the morning and evening when you are brushing your teeth, you can contemplate your goals, refresh them in your mind and think of ways to achieve them.

If we are reminded of something enough times, it motivates us to action, to transform ideas into reality. Transform one thing into another and something small into something larger.

If you have received this card it is a reminder to set reminders. Make sure you can see your goals.
Make sure you write them down as many times a day as you can. Even if its on your notes page in your phone.

Some people write them in their shower steam, on the door of the shower, on the wall of the shower.

I even spell them out when I'm jogging in the morning. I'm sure passers by think I'm quite mad, but I think I would rather be seen as rich and eccentric than poor and sound of mind.

Besides, during a monotonous exercise routine, isn't it a good use of time to focus on your goals. Repeat them often and feel energised and focused by them.
I also play team sports from time to time. This is not a good time to spell out your goals or think about anything other than the ball coming toward you.

But if you are walking, jogging, rowing or engaged in a solitary pursuit of some kind, by all means use this time to reinforce your goals. Anchor in the idea into your psyche that you are going to achieve great things.

Help your subconscious mind to understand this is happening, that it needs to help you to achieve greatness you and your business need to evolve into the beautiful butterfly that you can be.

The subconscious mind prefers symbols and stories and it can understand the written symbol or visual much better than an abstract concept.

If you tell your subconscious mind you want to be wealthy it will not understand. It might even think that you are already wealthy. It cannot bring you 'wealthy'. It can however bring you another '£1000' into your bank account. Tell it exactly what you want and it will bring it to you.

My husband and I anchor in good experiences all the time. We start each work day with the same saying. 'It is a beautiful day to make money' We always high five on this sentence. It never gets old, it always sparks joy in our lives. It always makes me laugh and sets the tone for our workday. The more cheesy it feels, the louder I laugh at our silliness.

Think of a great sentence or goal to start each day with and you will be amazed at the progress you start to make. Think of each day as a beautiful bright sparkling butterfly (some butterflies only live for one day) and think about how much you can achieve in one day. Be grateful that you have today and the bounty of benefits from today that you can use to progress your business and your abundance goals.

If you don't have anyone to 'high-five' with, please post your high-five at www.facebook.com/abundancemagic

If we can, we will high five you back at BST. You can also witness here, the hundreds of abundant beautiful sensitive souls out there giving their 'high fives' to an awesome abundant day.

When I first set up this page, I wondered how many people would engage in a 'high five', would it feel too cheesy? Would it take off? And now we have hundreds of followers 'high-fiving' from all over the globe.

We live in such an exciting time and I am so pleased to be a part of your world and share this joyous 'high five' moment. The moment each day when I check the 'high five' page, it lifts my energy and inspires me to share more, live more abundantly and grow exponentially more abundant. Sometimes it's important to tell others about your goals. This can be a hugely motivating action to take.

The butterfly card tells you it's time to set your goals free into the world. Tell your clients and the world that you are just about to put your prices up. This will spark action among those who were thinking about using your product or service. This is a very exciting energetically charged thing to do. It doesn't matter if you are not quite ready yet. Jut do it anyway and you will see how motivated you are to move heaven and earth to achieve your goal.

When I was painting these cards and writing this book, I told one person and then another and then another that the launch date for the book was Summer 2019, boy did that light a rocket under me to get the job done!

There were times of course when I felt I wouldn't reach my goal, but I buckled down and got moving, I cancelled all non-essential family and friend gatherings and evolved the book from the chrysalis stage into a beautiful book butterfly.

MONEY INSIGHTS:

1. You are a beautiful, bright soul, shine so that the whole world can see you
2. Make your goals visible to you all day
3. Anchor in good experiences
4. Count your blessings. Look at your bank account everyday. Count how much money you receive on a daily basis

GIRAFFE

*Uniqueness, self-love,
self-acceptance.*

*Forgive yourself
and others!*

21

GIRAFFE

The graceful giraffe reminds us to look above the trivial and trying problems that occur in business which try to block our abundance and wealth.

Rise above negativity. Rise above your own personal blocks and self sabotaging behaviours toward receiving money and financial abundance.

If you have pulled this card, you may be struggling with some repetitive behaviour of self sabotage.

Do you get just so far along your wealth journey and then find yourself back where you started?

The reality is, no matter how positive the other cards tell us to be, or how inspired we feel at one time in our businesses, we can come crashing down to earth and feel like we hit a brick wall.

Giraffe is here to remind you to take heart, that there

are lots of ways to prevent us from self sabotaging. The first step of course is to recognise that it happens.

Recognise the behaviour and the pattern and then we can do something about it.

What does abundance self sabotage look like:

- You self-generate stress. For example, you start more projects than you have time to finish.
- You work on low priority tasks, but leave high priority tasks undone.
- You overwork when what you really need is to step back and see the big picture. Ask a friend or confidant for help.
- You're self-critical when self-acceptance and compassion would have a more positive impact on your behaviour and emotions.
- You hold back from investing or otherwise taking charge of your money, because of shame and anxiety about a bad decision or experience from years ago.
  For example, you made a poor investment decision in your 20s. Now you're in your 30s and too scared to invest again.
- You overpay for items due to risk aversion. For example, you could buy generic version of a product for a fraction of the cost of brand-name, but you overpay for a sense of security.
- You will overpay for minimal extra gain. For example, you'll spend more for a top-of-the-line model when the extra features that model offers are not even particularly important to you.

- You make financial decisions based on being sucked into marketing incentives when those decisions don't make logical sense. For example, you'll pay more to stay at a hotel that belongs to a particular chain, because you collect their loyalty points, when realistically the points are only worth a fraction of the extra you paid.
- You keep paying for subscriptions you rarely use.

The SECOND STEP
Is to forgive yourself for past sabotaging behaviour.

PHYSICAL

It's quite simple. Not super easy but super simple:
1. Write down all your self sabotaging behaviours and fears about money.
2. Clear your self sabotaging behaviour by forgiving yourself and anyone else you can think of that caused you suffering around the money subject.
3. Say out loud either to the person or just by yourself that you forgive them
4. Repeat this mantra when you think you are about to self sabotage: 'I am sorry this happened, I forgive you, I love you, I have moved on'

METAPHYSICAL

If you are good at meditating then download the amazing money forgiveness meditation that you can:

www.abundance-magic.co.uk/forgiveness

MONEY INSIGHTS:

1. Recognised self sabotaging behaviour
2. Forgive yourself and others
3. Rise above negativity around money blocks

GEESE

Bravery, valour,
loyalty.

Forgive yourself and others!

22

GEESE

Geese are magical and beautiful creatures. They are quite large birds and during migration season, if a goose becomes injured, another goose will break free from the flock to stay behind and be with the injured or fallen goose. This is an incredible display of valour, devotion, and loyalty.

If you have pulled this card, it's time to take a good hard look at your 'family formation'. Does your family all fly together in a set pattern. Do you repeat the same money behaviours, all the time?
Do members of your family complain about money all the time? Do you have a family money motto?

My mum always says 'money comes in one hand and goes out the other'
or 'Money doesn't grow on trees'

Do your family members have sayings about money that they share with you constantly?

You might be being too loyal and devoted to keeping the 'family formation' alive.

Well intentioned ancestors often pass on their fears and troubles around money. They pass on lots of good habits and good genes and good DNA, (they survived all sorts of climates, world wars and diseases, after all), but they may accidentally pass on some big, fat, ugly fears around receiving money.

Sometimes they try to protect their offspring from the lack of money by teaching them to go without. They teach you how to be thrifty and they teach you to believe that you are happy living the life of a church mouse. This is fine if you are happy to live a life of normality but what if you want to break out of this formation?

What if you truly believe you should be wealthy?

How will you break formation and migrate to a sunnier climate?

Understanding the problem in the first place is really important. It's a difficult formation to break, because your whole family probably reinforces it all the time.

Every family gathering or even telephone conversation could include well used family 'quotes'. You could be extremely loyal to your family, which let's face it, most cultures drum this into our heads, and for good reason, it has helped your family to survive throughout the centuries so it's good to be loyal to family in some ways.

Let's break the problem down into the bits that aren't useful, the bits that hold you back, keep you small and stop you from living your 'magical, wonderfully abundant, fabulous, money miracle life'.

Example:
In your family life as a young child you would have witnessed the family dynamic around money. If this was less than stellar it could have made a big impression on your subconscious mind. This is the part of your mind that is programmed to help you in a fight or flight situation. It would have also affected your 'inner child' (read more about this in chapter 11 'TRUTH')

There is evidence all around you as a child that this is how your family 'is', this is 'the normal way to deal with money' this is what your family 'does with money', it 'struggles against poverty'. You could have developed all kinds of fears and resentments around money, you may have heard your parents arguing about money.

This conditioning doesn't just come from your parents, it comes from their parents and their parent's parents.

So going back generations upon generations your DNA and your subconscious brain may have been coded with information that you are meant to live a life of poverty.

YOUR CONSCIOUS BRAIN

Your conscious brain, however, can decide that after growing up without excess money that it will do what it can to change these circumstances. You might decide that you are not going to be like your parents. You go to University, get a degree, find an awesome job, climb the corporate ladder and earn a good salary. For a while and then. You start to 'self sabotage'. You identify that you are living a life way better than your parents lives. And you can start to feel guilty and feel like it might be better to get back into formation.

Chapter 4 deals with self-sabotage head on.

HOW TO RECONCILE WITH YOURSELF.

1. Make sure that you make small incremental changes so that your subconscious doesn't get scared and panic and self sabotage.

2. Start looking at your bank balance everyday
Start recording all the money you do make. This helps anchor into your subconscious mind the idea that you are worthy because people are paying you money. There is physical evidence that you are worthy and that you are worth it.

3. Encourage everyone in your family to improve their money mindset. Help them to start saying positive quotes about money.

4. Forgiving yourself and your family members for their attitudes and teachings around money will go a long way to helping you break formation and head towards your goals.

5. Put dates in your diary right now for 12 weeks time

and come back to the exercise and review how well you have done.

A friend was telling me recently that his mum used to tell him that 'a pound in your pocket is your best friend' Using the words 'money' and 'friend' in the same sentence has a higher vibrational feel than my family's motto: 'comes in one hand, goes out the other'. However, he did go on to explain to me that to him, this saying meant that people would be friends with him because he has money.

I have changed my money motto to:
'money loves me' which feels even better.

For those of you who like to meditate or who have found meditation serves you well to improve your circumstances then we have created an abundance mediation for you:

Doing this exercise will help to free you from the never ending cycle.
www.abundance-magic.co.uk/forgiveness

MONEY INSIGHTS:

1. Set boundaries and keep them in place
2. BREAK FORMATION that was set by your parents and their parents and their parent's parents.
3. Make small changes to improve your life every day

240

KINGFISHER

Peace, prosperity, balance.

Anchoring in positive experiences!

23

KINGFISHER

The Kingfisher is a symbol for abundance and wealth. A symbol of a fertile harvest and good fortune. If you feel like you are attracting negativity into your life, then the kingfisher is a great omen. It can change your fortune for the better.

The kingfisher, is also about finding a balance between work and play.

If you have been burning the candle at both ends it may be time to take a moment for yourself. This can be a couple of hours or a couple of days, just give yourself some time to stop and smell the roses, or to just 'be'.

I have often benefited from taking a break. If I am stuck on a problem or issue, or if the process feels long and laborious, I have been known to stop completely. Go do something else, make a meal, chat to a friend, go shopping, go for a walk, jog, run. Or even go to sleep and set the alarm to wake up early to carry on with the project. 9 times out of 10 I will have broken the 'spell' of repetition or spell of 'stuck' energy. I come back to the project with a fresh mindset and new focus and energy. The project often flies to the finish line and once again we achieve greatness!

Kingfisher also reminds us not to be afraid of new experiences. Have faith in the process. If you have been thinking of making some changes, now is the time to take action.

Anchoring in positive experiences.

Kingfisher reminds us to anchor in positive experiences.

Think about all the times you have anchored in bad experiences into your life. Every time something bad happens can you hear your self saying things like:

- That is so typical, another bad experience
- Bad things happen to good people
- Why do bad things always happen to me
- I should have know that the universe would bring me more bad luck

So if you have done this for years and years, it is time to lift that anchor up out of despair and set your sights on a far more positive journey. Find a sunny place where you can perch and focus on positive, happy things.

It takes time to change. And during the time that you are changing you may slip back into negativity. However, if this card keeps coming up, take heart, you are nearly in the clear, keep saying positive things and the universe will respond.

You will have to make a conscious decision to be happy. You will have to change your behaviour. You will need a pattern interrupter and you will need to start saying things like:

- Wow, the universe really does have my back
- I am a positive person and I look for positive experiences
- The world is a good place, most people are good.

Remember happiness is a choice.

This is why it is so important to high five or count the money as it comes into your experience.

Your subconscious is paying very close attention to your every command. It wants to bring you more of what you tell it you expect it to bring.

Therefore, if it sees you are counting money and sees you high five your business partner or your business mentor and say wow... I have really turned a corner, I am getting in more money than I thought I was, your subconscious will scurry around like crazy to bring you more of the same.

Read Chapter 5 'ACKNOWLEDGE' for more help on anchoring in your positive experiences.

MONEY INSIGHTS

1. Start a new journey today, right now.
2. Trust your instincts
3. Anchor in positive experiences
4. Happiness is a choice

DEER

*Luck, success,
regeneration.*

*If it isn't beautiful
or useful, it must go!*

24

DEER

The deer can show up when you are feeling a bit weary, if you feel like the hill is to high to climb, your goals feel far away and you feel like it's all too difficult.

Perhaps you feel like you have bitten off more than you can chew. Your eyes were bigger than your belly.

Or you may feel like a deer caught in the headlights. Frozen in place because you are either not sure what to do next or there is too much to do and you don't know where to start.

Are you stumbling blindly through the forest, not really knowing which way to turn?

This is a big sign from the universe that its time to DECLUTTER your thought process. We can as humans get caught up in the negativity around us.

Think about the news we hear on the radio, or the

headlines on newspapers. It's all sensationalism and negative agendas to keep people interested in buying and reading newspapers.

If you are in a state of low energy or feeling like life is a bit difficult, it could be time to stop listening to the news or keep it to a minimum.

I personally am so sensitive that listening to the news on the radio or watching it on television has a huge impact on me. I get caught up in the drama and my energy plummets. I need to be surrounded by sunshine and positive energy all the time.

I haven't listened to the news in years. Anything really important is brought up in conversation with friends and family, they often cannot wait to tell me all about it, so I don't need to listen to the negative opinions of other journalists all day, everyday. I have filtered them out of my experience.

PHYSICALLY

One of the best ways to DECLUTTER your mind is to list all the things that you are grateful for.

It might feel like a stretch to start writing down positive thoughts about what you are grateful for when you feel so downtrodden and weak.

The great thing about this exercise, however, is it soon helps you feel more positive and strong.

Stop reading right now and write down 5 financial things that you are grateful for, that perhaps you have previously taken for granted.

Examples:

- Your skills and knowledge in your field
- Your ability to think of great business ideas
- The amount of work you can get done in a day
- Business contacts that refer work to you
- Any money you have received for your product or service so far

This exercise is very uplifting. I love it so much and I felt such a marked improvement when I did it that I made it a part of my every day habits. At 9 pm every night I have my Google calendar send me a reminder that says: 'I am so grateful for all that I have and all that I have achieved today... #blessed'

I am pleased to report that since I have had this reminder every night, I have doubled my achievements on a daily basis. I am far more effective in my business and I get heaps more done. I thought I was pretty effective and efficient in the business, but my subconscious mind has shown me how much more I can achieve with the right mindset!

NEXT
Declutter your business. This is a great tool to use when you are feeling a bit flat or low.

Plan to declutter your whole life. One draw or box at a time but it is CRITICAL that you start with your business.

- Declutter your desk, pack away anything that doesn't need to be there.
- Next tackle files or folders or boxes of stuff. Sift through everything and throw out all the old bits of paper, broken paper clips, dog eared post it notes, broken pens, elastic bands and anything that isn't magical. If it doesn't spark joy in your life it has to go. If it isn't beautiful or useful get rid of it.
- A great show to watch for inspiration is 'Tidying up with Marie Kondo' she has a book out too.

The reality is, if you have clutter in your life, it is very difficult for beautiful magical energy to come into your experience. The same can be said for your business.

Develop a system for your workflow. Make sure if anyone asks for anything, you can find it quickly and easily. I want you to spend your time on uplifting, interesting tasks, not sifting through piles of junk trying to find something.

By having a business springclean, you can release stuck energy and allow the magic of wealth to flow into your experience.

METAPHYSICALLY

We have a fabulous meditation for you to download

on this subject. It only takes a few minutes and it is guaranteed to lift your vibration and put you back in the driving seat.

www.abundance-magic.co.uk/DECLUTTER

MONEY INSIGHTS:

1. Declutter your business
2. Set a reminder about how grateful you are
3. Make sure you are recording how much money comes into your business... everyday!

RABBIT

*Speed, abundance,
fertility...*

*Count every penny
you receive!*

25

RABBIT

Apart from being able to reproduce very quickly, rabbits are known for their speed and they have long ears which can be as long as 10 cm.

If you have pulled this card then you need to receive a message about listening.

Are you listening to your instincts?

Do you have a hunch about something?

If you do have an idea about how to start a new business or write a book or start a program, the rabbit card is spurring you on.

Listen to your hunches and act quickly. In her book 'Big Magic', Elizabeth Gilbert talks about the idea that big ideas don't hang around forever. If you don't act fast, it won't be long before you see your big idea with someone else's name attached to it.

This idea can be applied to smaller goals or changes that you might need to make to your business. Trust your hunches and instincts. Look at ways of improving systems, products, processes and tell your clients and prospective clients all about them.

I do go on about this and it features in most cards, because its so important:

Count how much money you receive on a daily basis. I guarantee you will be surprised and if you are not already doing this then start right now.

I don't care if you write your earnings on a piece of paper. Or in a beautifully bound leather book. Or on our APP. Download abundance magic APP. and start counting your pennies.

The important thing is that you do it. Show the universe how grateful you are. Show the universe that you care. That you are awake, that you want to be taken seriously.

It isn't just me saying this, all the wonderful people on our website and in our MONEY INSIGHTS group agree.

As soon as they start counting their money they start to recognise how well they are doing and the cycle continues to improve and they start making more money. Their money starts reproducing like bunny rabbits.

Read more about instincts in Chapter 1 'INSTINCTS'

If you would like to talk to like minded people about your goals or hopes and dreams,
join us at
www.abundance-magic.co.uk/MONEYINSIGHTS

MONEY INSIGHTS:

1. Trust your hunches and instincts
2. Act quickly
3. Make sure you are recording how much money comes into your business...everyday!

CRAB

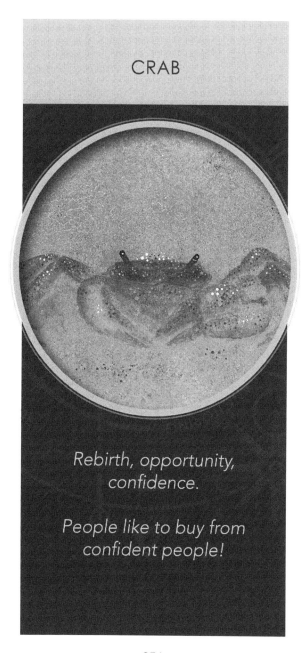

*Rebirth, opportunity,
confidence.*

*People like to buy from
confident people!*

26

CRAB

Crabs are known as shy creatures, disappearing often inside their shells. Since crabs cast off their shells after a certain period of time, many cultures have linked this behaviour to rebirth and a new start in life.

If you are shy like I am, you may be self-sabotaging your financial abundance. Hiding away from opportunities that the universe brings right to you. There may be many opportunities for you to grow your business, improve your sales and change your financial situation, if only you could get your claws into them.

Having been brought up in a shy family. I inherited these shy traits and all the difficulties that go along with this characteristic.

I wasn't a good public speaker, I have had to force myself to speak to people, in order to improve and grow my business. I taught myself to stand up in front of a room full of people and tell them who I am and what my business is about.

I don't know if anyone can truly understand how terrified I was the first time I had to speak publicly. I was trembling and shaking and felt completely out of my comfort zone.

Traditionally throughout my life, whenever I had to speak, even if it was just to my classmates at school, I would experience all the classic fear symptoms:

My mouth would dry up completely and I would lose focus as well as the thread of what I was talking about. Instead of the well prepared speech running through my mind, I would instead see, what I can only describe as millions of tiny white specks in front of me. I couldn't see the audience at all. I would see lots of dots, as though the air had become a thick mass of white dots, enveloping the audience, their eyes are the only thing that remain, staring holes into the deepest parts of my soul. Judging me!

Whatever speech I had spent time memorising disappeared completely from my mind as though it had never entered my brain in the first place.

No matter how well I knew my subject, or how much I practiced the speech, it would always be a frustrating flop.

I would say lots of 'uhmmms' etc. My hands would shake uncontrollably, I couldn't hold a piece of paper as it made the shaking seem so much more obvious.

One of the things I did to help my shyness was enrol in my local Toastmasters group. The first couple of meetings all the usual symptoms showed up ...

And one of the most annoying self-sabotaging things that I have traditionally done is to try to get out of attending the event at the last minute. My conscious brain has a massive wobbly fit and comes up with a million excuses as to why I shouldn't attend the meeting.

Wow! The very thing I needed more than anything in the world to help grow my business. And I would try talk myself out of it. That's taking self-sabotage to the next level. I pass that class with honours!.

It has taken sheer willpower to get in my car and drive to the event and speak in front of the friendliest, nicest bunch of people you could hope to meet.

So what is that all about?
Do you have similar experiences?
Are there things you do to self-sabotage?

PHYSICAL SOLUTION

The physical solution is to keep on going to Toastmasters. Or an equivalent confident speakers group.

Even though I'm the shyest person I know, by the 4th or 5th time I attended Toastmasters I started to relax a bit into it. I found 'my grove'. I found 'my voice' and 'my presentation style'.

I can guarantee that if you attend a group that helps with public speaking regularly, and take on board the feedback that they give you and just try your best, you will start to see a marked improvement in your ability to speak publicly.

I would never in a million years believe that I personally could change on such a fundamental level. And yet, I am living proof that it can be done.

I set myself the goal to be so confident at public speaking that I would be able to speak anywhere or anytime.

Even really good speakers attend our Toastmasters group. Even though they are 'great speakers', they too have to practice to remain good at speaking. Just like a doctor or a yoga teacher 'practices' their vocation, a speaker needs to continue practicing to remain good or great at speaking.

The reality is that people like to 'buy' from confident people. They want to know that you are good at what you do and that they are 'buying into' your brand for all the right reasons.

If you are a bit shy and not that confident in a boardroom or pitch setting where you have to present your products or services, you may lose the sale to someone who is a lot more confident than you are.

I think you owe it to yourself to address the issue and improve your chances of making a sale.

METAPHYSICAL SOLUTION.

We have created a meditation exercise for you to download on the website. This is an exercise that you can do before any public speaking engagement, including presenting to any new clients or any event that you attend. It will help you to ground yourself, and activate your abundance magic, and ultimately channel your most magical abundant self.

To access the meditation go to:
www.abundance-magic.co.uk/MEETINGSPACE

MONEY INSIGHTS:

1. Self-sabotage comes in many formats. Review any areas where this is happening in your business
2. Improve your public speaking abilities. People buy from confident people
3. Practice makes perfect
4. Prepare for meetings and ground yourself

FROG

Wealth, fertility, abundance.

Stick with your goals!

27

FROG

It's a sticky business!

If you have pulled this card from the deck it is a reminder or an alert from your subconscious mind that you need to put your heart and soul into something.

Stick with your goals and make the changes you need to ensure you succeed.

Are you a bit of a tumble weed at the moment?

I was born in the star sign of Aquarius (which is no excuse) but it does mean I can be a bit fickle or flaky some times. I tend to go with the flow too often, adopting other people's agendas. Getting caught up in their needs and wants.

For example, years ago, if my mum was catering an event that weekend, I would be pulled in to help with the prep and set everything up. I'd be slicing and dicing from sun up to sun down!

And of course, if I had nothing else going on, then that is a great way to spend time with a family member, learn a skill, or generally help.

However, if you find you are constantly putting other people's needs before your own, then it is time to set some boundaries.

My husband and I live in one of the loveliest villages imaginable, and the friends we have made almost overnight are great. However, I work from home a lot, and just because I'm at home, doesn't mean I'm available to get involved in all sorts of events, dramas, volunteering efforts etc.

I have put down some serious boundaries for my wonderful friends, family and neighbours. They have a very clear understanding that at times I am not available, I am at work 'building my empire'.

Your personal wealth accrual and money itself is an entity that needs your full attention. If you stick to your goals and persevere you will be triumphant.

The frog is here to remind you about metamorphosis from egg to tadpole and finally the adult frog. Think about what you can do in your business, what products or services are you offering that could be transformed into something better.

Or is it your marketing that needs to be adjusted,

evolved into a better, improved version. Have you used the same advert for years?

If it is truly working then of course, stick with it, but if you feel sales are dwindling, a refresh could be the answer to get your sales targets met.

If you are feeling stuck on this subject, you may need to do some de-cluttering in your business.

The subject of de-cluttering is covered extensively in the Chapter 7 - DECLUTTERING of this book. However, if you have picked the frog card, then you may need to hop on over to a mini declutter session to get over some stuck energy around something in your business.

Decluttering physical stuff around your desk or office is always a good thing, however, you may need to do some administrative decluttering too.

Are your employees or suppliers worth their weight in gold?

If not, consider making some changes right about now.

I am as loyal as the next person, but you are the captain of the ship, if your ship 'sinks' or 'sails' it is down to your personal decisions.

The onus is on you to make your business work, hit the sales targets and amass your abundance and wealth.

Sometimes you have to be a bit ruthless and change

suppliers, systems, processes or procedures etc. to ensure you stay afloat.

Setting boundaries for suppliers and staff is a critical part of being in business. If they don't know what is expected of them, both staff and suppliers can waste time and energy on the wrong tasks. This can be incredibly demotivating too, so make sure you have a clear understanding of what everyone is meant to be doing.

If you are lucky enough to have a team of people working for you, make sure they each have a clearly defined job role. Make sure the company ethos is clearly available for all the team to see.

In the past, when I worked for other people, I used to feel really frustrated if I felt like I was set up to fail.

I treated each company I worked for as if it were my own, and if the line of communication was murky, and I wasn't able to feel like I was making progress, I would get extremely impatient and frustrated.

This can have a ripple effect, if one member of staff is frustrated, it can bring others down too.

MONEY INSIGHTS:

1. Set up boundaries
2. Make sure staff and suppliers have a clear understanding of what is expected of them
3. Declutter your service, product or marketing

ZEBRA

Individuality, freedom, uniqueness.

Is everything always black and white? Embrace the grey areas!

28

ZEBRA

Zebra reminds us you that there is more than one way to look at a problem.

If you are stuck on a problem, ask the audience or phone a friend... by changing your thought process, you could find the answer to the problem.

Not everything is black and white. For some people it is quite easy to see the world in black and white.
They have no 'grey areas'.

Most of us however, need the grey areas. We need to take a million little steps toward our goals. The good news of course, is that the little steps soon add up and with practice, we gain momentum and soon we are on our way to victory.

Why is it important to take one step at a time?

Do you want to run before you can walk?

It's very natural to want to do so, and of course you do need to aim high. But if you run before you walk, you could fall flat on your face.

The best way to achieve big things is by doing small things to get there. One of the most important things you can do is change your habits.

Do you have a habit of saying or thinking negative things about your finances? Do you hear others say these things often?

I totally understand this bad habit. I had a poor habit of sorting out my finances last, putting them off to the end of the day/week/month.

I would far rather do any other task to do within my business than sort out the finances. I would even rather do 'admin' than finances.

As soon as I made the shift to putting the finances first, however, things changed. It was difficult at first, but it was the best thing I could have done for my business. I can pretty much guarantee that all successful businesses have a strong financial foundation.

The problem with so many entrepreneurs and new business owners is that they tend to be 'technicians' first and financially aware last. And artistic, sensitive people like myself seem to operate on the opposite end of the scale to financially minded folk. We may know our product or service inside out and back to front. We may give our clients a five star service, we may be phenomenal at every other part of the business but if we don't back this all up with good financial habits then all could be lost.

The very first sentence to this book is
'You teach best, what you most need to learn'

I have always loved this saying because I know how true it is. By teaching this subject, I have learned to embrace it and am better off for it.

Reasons why we have habits.

Our brains are actually wired to subsume a lot of the daily things we need to do in order to free up other parts of the brain which can then focus on interesting or important projects.

By following a certain routine everyday, getting dressed the same way, eating the same breakfast, we take a lot of decision making out of the equation.

It means we can be thinking about something else, whilst we are on auto pilot getting the boring chores done.

In order to change our habits we need to embrace 'alternatives'. Alternatives are the key to making lasting change.

Taking control of your habits and changing them is very powerful. Because these habits accumulate day after day into outcomes that can be very significant.

If you have a bad habit around money, list the alternative habits now on a piece of paper or in your journal. These are the key to producing long lasting effective change.

What's behind it all?

The reason some of our habits around money exist, is because we have a fear of the alternative.

So if for example you don't enjoy looking at your bank balance every day, this could be because it reminds you that you don't have enough money in it (fear).

Some people in our money mindset group tell me that 'they don't want to be burdened with looking at the bank balance every day, they feel it is extreme to have to do this every single day'.

My suggestion to them then, is that they have not really understood the alternative.

Of course this is a habit that needs to change because if you don't look at your bank balance every day and you don't count how much money is coming in everyday, then your subconscious gets lazy and doesn't do what it needs to do, to get you earning more money.

The outcome of not looking at your bank balance everyday would be that you don't see the iceberg below the surface and you carry on steering your ship into a disaster and end up bankrupt and going out of business.

Would you rather face your small fear today of looking at your bank balance and doing something about it?
Or
Would you like to face a massive fear of going bankrupt and having to tell people, including yourself that you didn't make it?

Can you agree with me now that facing your fear of looking at the bank balance is a great option? We should be grateful that we have this option available.

If you have a bad habit think of the alternatives.
Is the frustration of living without the abundance of wealth you deserve not worth breaking your bad habit?

If you want to change your perspective think of the consequences of your actions.

Create a list of alternatives.

List all the things you could do to
- create more wealth
- grow your business
- market your services
- market your products

If you are in the habit of doing the same thing over and over again, think of alternatives. What else could you do to create more wealth?

Get into the good habit of facing your small fears about a public speaking opportunity rather than a large fear of outright failure.

Build up your habits slowly, with purpose. You will be so glad you did.

You can read more about this in Chapter 9 - 'ALTERNATIVES'

MONEY INSIGHTS:

1. Face your fears and get into good habits
2. There is more than one way to look at a problem
3. Everything is not black and white

RAM

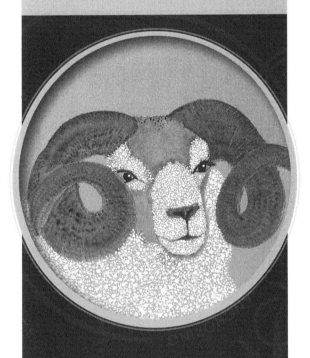

Sensitivity and perseverance.

A time for new beginnings!

29

RAM

Aries astrological sign, is symbolized by the strong ram. As the first sign of the Zodiac, Aries the ram symbolizes leadership and authority.

Bighorn sheep have split hooves with rough bottoms, which improve their grip on rocky terrain, they only need a two-inch space to gain a foothold. This means sheep can climb mountains using opportunistic 'ledges' that are easily missed by others or passed on by those who don't have the courage to take the risk of falling.

On those days when you think you just don't know where to step, look for even the tiniest opportunity and make the leap. Sheep energy will be there to make sure you are on solid ground.

The ram's horns are effective and dangerous, however, the horns grow in a spiral which is symbolic of eternity.

Do you have some ideas spiralling around in your head?

If you find it difficult to put thoughts down on paper or you don't have the right people in your immediate circle to talk to, it would be worth joining a mastermind group who can be a great sounding board for your ideas.

We have a MONEY INSIGHTS group online that you can join if you would like to share your thoughts and receive valuable money insights from other like minded business owners.

www.abundance-magic.co.uk/MONEYINSIGHTS

During fights, bighorn rams may throw themselves at their opponents at speeds of up to 20 miles per hour. If you have picked this card, it's time to charge toward your goals. Harness the energy of the ram and headbutt your way through any negativity or problems. Take some risks and take charge!

If you have some steep money goals to get to then you will have to head but your way through some tough decisions and break up any fears you have that get in your way.

The ram energy is all about 'I am, therefore I am' You don't need to make excuses about who you are and what you are doing. You don't need anyone's permission.

You are who you are and you are allowed to be who you are. You are not an accident. If you want the whole world to like you before you get out there and make your idea public, then you will wait forever. You don't need the whole world to like you, you just need to identify with your target market.

Another message from the ram:

Bighorn ewes give birth during the spring, and hide their lambs on narrow, rocky ledges at high elevations in order to keep them from wolves, mountain lions, bears, and coyotes. The lesson we can learn from these wily sheep is to look at our own conduct of business.

Are we being smart about our finances? Could we put some money on a ledge out of the way for a rainy day?

These sheep climb cliffs diagonally in a Z shape in order to reduce the steepness of each step and preserve strength.

Are there systems and procedures that you could introduce into your business to preserve energy?

By automating some tasks you can free up your time to do other more important tasks and keep your attention on your goals.

MONEY INSIGHTS:

1. Take some risks and take charge
2. Save some money for a rainy day
3. Automate tasks in your business

HIPPOPOTAMUS

Courage, calm, strength.

Stay positive and strong!

30

HIPPOPOTAMUS

Hippopotamus is a symbol of strength, teaching us courage and calmness in the face of adversity.

I'm sure, like myself, you have read or listened to or watched lots of interesting people talk about spirituality and abundance and the secret to a better life.

They all talk about the fact that you need to stay positive in order to receive the beautiful abundant gifts that this world can offer. And that is true, I agree with that statement, but what they don't tell you is how to get there. Especially in the face of adversity. What do you do when your whole world is falling apart around you?

How do you stay positive and strong?

They also talk about how energy follows thought. So if you have spent many years thinking negative thoughts and telling yourself negative things then it can be difficult to just suddenly adopt a sunny disposition toward money. It can be really irritating to feel like a failure because everyone around you is laughing and joyous and seems to be living a charmed life, whilst you feel downtrodden and like you are a heavyweight, living in a pit of never ending despair.

Even when you have been living a positive life for some time you can still fall off the well positioned pedestal and find yourself hurtling headlong into a downer.

I remember opening a letter from one of the accounts I had and realised that I hadn't been paying off as much as I thought I had. For some reason, not sure if I was just feeling a bit down before I opened the mail but for some reason I felt myself spiralling downward.

I wished that I had prepared myself mentally and emotionally before I had opened the mail. In some ways because my life had been so blessed and positive and happy for such a long time, the downward spiral seemed to feel that much more intense.

What to do about it:

The most important thing I can tell you right now is that you need to find a system that works for you. Everyone is different.

I am a huge fan of mini-meditations.
I love big, long meditations and do some as I'm falling asleep but also love little ones that I do during the day. (Not whilst driving of course) but most other times of

the day, even a few minutes in front of the computer can be a complete game changer. They raise my vibrational energy and give me strength and insight to cope with all kinds of challenges.

Your system for getting back on track could be physical or metaphysical. Helpful, practical guide listed below.

PHYSICALLY

1. Spend time with positive friends and relatives. Talking to others about your feelings can help us to process them, put them into perspective, and obtain advice and support.

2. You could be overwhelmed at this particular time in your life or in your business or financial journey. Break down large tasks into smaller ones, and set realistic deadlines for completing them.

3. Do things that you enjoy. Even if its a guilty pleasure. No one needs to know.

4. Get out of the house, or office even if it is just a short walk round the block. Bright light, fresh air, and the hustle and bustle can change your perspective.

5. Make a list of all the positive things about yourself and your business. However bad you may be feeling, remember that you have not always felt this way, and will not always feel this way.

6. Be realistic about your progress. Improvements in

mood are likely to be gradual rather than sudden, and you may even get worse before you start getting better.

7. Sleep on it. Avoid making important decisions straight away. This would include things like leaving your job, firing a staff member, or spending a large amount of money. A fresh mind after a good nights sleep will help you gain perspective, get you feeling positive again.

8. I am not a psychologist or doctor, I can give you lists of things to do to improve your mood and keep you feeling positive, however, if things go on too long, then seek specialist advice via your doctor. You could ask for counselling and then take things from there.

I also suggest that you read chapter 10's lessons about taking responsibility. It will help you on your journey to wealth and abundance.

METAPHYSICALLY

101 ways to feel positive. We have created a soundtrack for you to listen to on our website that will put a smile on your face and take you out of your downward spiralling feelings.

101 ways to feel positive and attract abundance by using the power of your subconscious mind.

www.abundance-magic.co.uk/101

MONEY INSIGHTS:

1. Surround yourself with positive people
2. Take responsibility for your own life
3. Break down large tasks into smaller ones and set realistic deadlines
4. Reward yourself with things that spark joy

COW

Generosity, selflessness, provision.

Energetic alignment with abundance and wealth!

31

COW

Cows are the embodiment of generosity and selflessness. Fertility, sustenance, abundance, potential, calming, grounding and provision.

Cows have been a great part of our lives for many years. They seem perfectly aligned with their duty to us humans.

They have manifested a life for themselves where they are taken care of by farmers, they can spend their days, chewing the cud and wandering in fields. Soaking up the sun and the good energies that mother earth has to offer.

How do we become energetically aligned to all the wealth and abundance that the sacred cow promises to deliver, how can we manifest abundance like a cow?

This may seem silly at first. The concept that I was not energetically aligned to money was a rather foreign idea when I first heard it.

My mind raced through my thought processes regarding money, wealth and abundance. I thought to myself:
Money is all I think about, I am constantly looking for new ways to make money, constantly thinking in terms of improving my wealth so why would I not be energetically aligned to money.
The idea seemed preposterous!

The truth of course, is that if you have spent many years in a situation where you are not wealthy and have had financial struggles then you may not be as energetically aligned to wealth and abundance as you think you are.

You may also have inherited a 'vow of poverty' from your family. You may be stuck in a cycle of poverty that has been handed down from generation to generation.

The way to find out of course is to look at your bank balance. If there is not much money in your bank account then it's a great indication that you are not aligned to the wealth you expect and desire. If the bank balance is way lower than you need it to be then you should consider adjusting your energetic alignment with your financial abundance.

The path to riches is not paved in gold, in my opinion it is paved in practice, practice, practice.

If you want to be great at something if you want to be a world class leader in your field, you need to practice.

This book you are holding in your hands and the associated cards will help you and show you the way forward. All you need to do is practice the lessons and you can start living your magical, abundant life.

I'm reminded here of the very famous quote by Jascha Heifetz, a Russian-American violinist. Many consider him to be the greatest violinist of all time:

'If I don't practice one day, I know it; two days, the critics know it; three days, the public knows it'. Jascha Heifetz

Similarly, I find, that if I neglect my finances for 2 or 3 days, the sales funnel dries up, the phone stops ringing, the emails go quiet and I look outside the window to make sure the world is still spinning as it should be, because I can actually feel the wheel of abundance stop spinning.

The good news is that its fairly simple to change. Not exactly easy but simple.

You need to practice changing your energy into alignment with money. All the cards in this deck are aimed at small parts of the whole system that will change your energy and align you with the magical abundant wealth that you deserve to have.

The reason why I invented these cards in the first place is because I get bored really easily.

I know that I have to practice these different aspects in order to improve my financial situation but I can't bear

288

the thought of doing the same thing over and over again.

I know logically and consciously that I have to do these things to improve my financial situation but I needed to find a way to conquer the boredom.

By picking 3 different cards every week, I break up the process and thereby focus on practicing 3 different aspects of improving my wealth and abundance and ultimately improve my energetic alignment with this wealth and abundance.

I also find that by channelling the different energies of the animals, I'm far more engaged with the process. My brain feels interested and excited to know which animal I'm going to pick next, I can't wait to get started on the lesson.

I have also noticed over time that my ability to connect with the animal energy improves exponentially, all the activities that I am doing gain momentum and my financial abundance has improved across the board.

I don't mind admitting that in the beginning, some of the subjects seemed all encompassing and I had to focus on one card for the week, however, as time passed and I started to PRACTICE the different lessons, it became easier and easier to set goals, stay focused and improve my financial abundance.

I also found that the more I could weave the lessons into my everyday experience the easier the goal was achieved.

Easy ways to bring the lessons into your everyday experience are things like changing your passwords to remind you of your goals.

Think about a few words that sum up your goals and use them as your password on your computer.
Pick a number to use as the password to unlock your phone and so on.

All the cards work together to get your subconscious on board and the universe starts to notice your new patterns and matches them with wonderful coincidences. You start showing up at just the right time, you start meeting just the right clients. Synchronisation unfolds in a beautifully, magical way.

I can't wait for your energetic alignment and positive wealth to grow.

If you have had an amazing synergistic experience after using these cards then please do tell us about it at: www.abundance-magic.co.uk/peacock.

MONEY INSIGHTS:

1. Align yourself energetically with wealth and abundance
2. Pull 3 cards every week and take small steps toward your financial goals
3. PRACTICE, PRACTICE, PRACTICE, and repeat

FLAMINGO

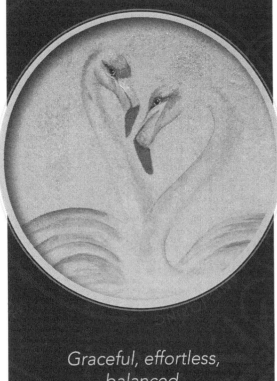

*Graceful, effortless,
balanced.*

*Well balanced communication
and energetic action!*

32

FLAMINGO

The flamingo is beautiful in it's stature and grace, able to stand on one foot effortlessly whilst keeping the other one tucked in to retain its body warmth.

Flamingo suggests that you be well-balanced in your COMMUNICATION and in ENERGETIC ACTIONS

'Energetic actions' are actions that you take with 'considered' thought and 'strategy' in mind. Much like the flamingo stands on one leg to conserve body heat, you need to adapt your business to bring in more business by taking 'energetic action' to do so.

Energetic actions might include traditional business activities ... but with a twist:

- Sales
- Advertising
- Marketing

And the twist: before you undertake any of these actions, think carefully about your target market. Put yourself in their shoes.

Example:
I had a new business approach me to design a website for their trophy and engraving company. The directors of the business were a mother and son team. When I was taking the brief for the design of the website, they couldn't agree on what the overall brand colouring should be.
After listening to them debating (heatedly) for a few minutes, I politely interjected and asked what they both thought that their target market would expect to see?

This changed their demeanour completely. They were both able to take their personal preference for colour out of the equation and settled on their best guess as to what a trophy companies' website colouring should look like.

If you drew this card from the pack its time to take energetic action. You need to refresh your marketing messages and get them out into the world.

You need to be graceful and memorable, like the flamingo, and once you get your marketing and sales messages right, your business growth will be effortless.

In this day and age, there are a lot of marketing media options to choose from.

I hear all the time from clients in my branding business

that some traditional marketing mediums no longer work.

I sincerely doubt this fact. Considering I work with many clients whose marketing is very effective and we use many traditional as well as modern methods to advertise their products and services.

That said, if something isn't working, then by all means change it, or change the message that you are sending out into the world. Change the design, the heading, the offering, the call to action, change anything and everything. Give your marketing, advertising, sales pitch the refresh that it needs to be effective in growing your business.

Getting the balance right is key. I work with a lot of clients who are so impatient, and because they have seen their own Facebook post 100 times that week, they think that their target market has seen it too... Not true!

Marketing takes time. Your target market needs to see your message between 7 and 12 times before they buy into the brand. Not 7 different messages. But rather the same message 7 times.

I am one of the most impatient people in the world, but even I know not to change too much, too quickly.

Experience has taught me that a well thought through marketing campaign can have a huge impact on your sales. But it does take time. Marketing is a slow, but effective tool.

TEST AND MEASURE. If you cannot test and measure the result of the marketing campaign then you could be wasting time and money. Make sure you have some way of recording the effectiveness of the campaign.

Adding a special code or unique email address to a set of marketing material means that you can continually assess the effectiveness of the campaign and adjust the strategy as and when you need to.

If you are not sure what to do or how to go about marketing your product or service, ask your peers to recommend a brand or marketing agency to help you with your campaign.

But whatever you do, make sure you do something. It's no good moping around, complaining that the phone isn't ringing, when you haven't tried to advertise or market your product or service.

If you prefer sales activities to marketing activities, then make sure you are getting out and about and telling people all about your products and services. Have you written a sales letter lately?

Have you booked speaking engagements?

I was one of the shyest people in the world when I started my branding business, and yet, no matter what, whenever I gave a talk on my subject, I always won new business. At least one new client, every time. So what are you waiting for? Get out there and start selling!

If you are standing around on both legs waiting for clients to contact you, you are wasting your time and energy... get comfortable, being uncomfortable. It may be uncomfortable or unfamiliar in the beginning but start standing on one leg and experience the results of this magical energetic action.

The flamingo card is a reminder to get out there and get talking and fill your calendar with speaking engagements. Ask colleagues if they know of anyone looking for a speaker. Sign up to any local exhibitions and ask if you can be the 10-minute speaker at local networking events. What are you waiting for? Do it now!

MONEY INSIGHTS:

1. Start a new marketing campaign
2. Book speaking engagements
3. Test and measure which energetic actions you have taken are working. And do more of them!

ORANGUTAN

Creation and
manifestation.

Stretch yourself
a little bit further!

33

ORANGUTAN

Orangutans measure 1.2m to 1.5m tall and weigh up to 100kg. And they have one seriously big arm span – some males can stretch their arms 2m from fingertip to fingertip!

Orangutan's message to us is to stretch our arms out to bigger business opportunities and bring in more wealth.

Whatever level you are at, could you stretch yourself a bit further.

STRETCH ONE

If you are living your life in first gear, you may be lazing about, waiting for the phone to ring, you are physically around, but you are not actually engaged in driving your business forward. You need to make time to work on your business, not just in it.

This may mean you need to employ someone to help

with the day to day running of the business, or help with the financial side of things. Or even an administrative assistant that can answer phones and emails and allow you to get on with planning, marketing and sales to drive the business forward.

STRETCH TWO

Shift into second gear, stretch those long arms even wider, could it be time to raise your prices? This can be a very uncomfortable thing to do. But think about it like this. If you have been in business for a while, you have more experience and that experience is worth more money than when you started out with little experience

.
You deserve to get a raise for all the hard work and dedication you have put into your business.
If you were an employee you would be expecting a raise right about now.

A great way to get started is to send out a marketing message to tell your clients that you are raising your prices on a certain date, you are bound to end up with a lot more orders in your inbox before that date arrives.

PS. It's important to mention that you need to be prepared for the onslaught of enquiries and have the capacity to fulfil the orders should this happen.
Brand damage is really difficult to undo. If customers find your service slow or inadequate you could lose them forever.

Also worth mentioning: If you lose some clients and

get a bit of flack about your prices from one or two people, recognise this as a 'rite of passage'. It can be uncomfortable and put you out of your comfort zone, especially if you are a sensitive person.

If you really struggle with this, talk to a trusted colleague about it, or a mentor find a safe way for you to tell someone what you are going through.

You may want to join our Money Mindset group, a group of like-minded individuals who will understand what you are going through.

www.abundance-magic.co.uk/moneymindset

STRETCH THREE

If you already have a marketing campaign in place then you need 'up the anti' and look at new ways of getting your message out to your target market. For example, try different mediums like mini videos which are effective on social media.

STRETCH FOUR

You may need to update your branding and/or your website to look appropriate and match to your new target market. If clients are spending more money on your product or service, they want to know that you look and act the part. This will give them confidence in buying into your brand.

STRETCH FIVE

Speaking engagements. As mentioned in the flamingo chapter, a speech will capture your target markets attention and give them a deeper understanding of who you are, what your products or service is and how it can help them and people they know to improve their lives.

I have mentioned in several parts of this book that I am not a 'salesperson', I was the opposite of a 'salesperson' and the opposite of a 'public speaker' when I started out and even I won new clients when I forced myself to speak at networking events.

If you know this works, then why isn't your diary filled with speaking engagements?

Get out there and ask everyone you know if they need a speaker. You will be so glad you did!

STRETCH SIX

Change the way you do business with existing and new clients.

One of the best ways to make money is by a monthly subscription. Or a programme.

One of the best things I ever did was offer my branding clients a 0% payment plan. They had to sign a contract, but they got all their design and marketing material up front and then they were able to pay for it over 6 to 12 months.

This helped me with cash flow in the early days and it was easier to plan when I knew what money was coming in. It helped my clients because all new fledgling businesses have loads of up front costs. It made it super easy for them to start their business and get the word out about their products and services.

Think about ways you can offer a subscription or a programme or 0% interest to your clients to help your business and theirs to move forward.

The monkey card talks about a passive income. Could you develop a set of materials, a course or something that could be sold online? Could you write a book about your subject?

Think about ways to ensure you have a steady income coming in.
Amazon have developed a great monthly package with their Audible offer. The small subscription fee gives you access to a new audible book every month. Audio books have changed my life. I've always loved being able to do two things at once. I can listen to a book on my morning jog or whilst I'm doing the grocery shopping (normally so boring) or whilst I'm planting or weeding at the allotment. It's just FAB!

Are there any products or services you could create that could help people, change their lives and earn you a constant stream of money every month?

STRETCH SEVEN

Are you energetically aligned to your new price model that you are expecting clients to sign up to?

The way that energy works in terms of alignment is an interesting phenomena. If you have a subscription for something or if you pay for goods/services via a payment plan, your energetic vibration around payment plans or monthly payments has a 'high', 'positive' vibration around it.

If you then ask your clients to pay you in monthly instalments, they will feel your 'high energetic vibration' on this subject and it will feel like a good match for them. They will feel positive about paying the monthly instalments.

If you have never had a subscription in your life, your energetic vibration around this subject could be quite low and your clients will feel this 'low vibration' and may feel a 'negative energy' around the subscription. If you have never paid for a course or bought a book or system or paid for products and services, why would you expect other people to do so?

I personally have subscriptions, I have bought into lots of products and services and my clients sense this, they find me an 'energetic match' to my service offerings and therefore they feel motivated to buy from me and my business in the form of a monthly instalment.

If you don't want to go down this route, if you don't

have any monthly instalments and you don't want to sell your product or service that way, that is fine. Stick to payments up front instead. I'm just saying that if you do want to sell and earn money on a monthly basis then you need to be an 'energetic match' to this concept.

The same principle applies for the actual 'price' you pay for goods/services. If you have only ever paid small amounts of money for things, if you only ever buy the cheapest product or services then your will have a 'low vibration' around 'high priced' products and services.

If you have paid for a course or product at a similar price to what you are selling, then you will have a 'high vibrational' energy around that price point. Your clients/customers will pick up on this energy and it will influence them one way or another.

If you want to change your vibration to be positive around 'high' priced items, you need to start updating everything in your life in a gradual manner. If you update or upgrade everything around you, consistently moving from one thing to another, it will help you become a better 'vibrational match' to 'higher priced' products and services. You will then be able to charge more for your products and services.

It is important to start small for two reasons, firstly, it's no good going into debt to update something, and secondly, it might be 'too much', 'too soon' for your subconscious mind to handle if you splurge out on an outrageously 'over priced' upgrades. You might go into debt or it might be too much of a jump and you could end up right back where you started, on a 'low vibrational match' to high priced items.

By updating or upgrading and refreshing things around you slowly and consistently, you give your subconscious mind some solid evidence that it is good to upgrade and it is a positive sign for your subconscious to continue to do so.

This is how you build wealth and abundance, 'slow and steady wins the race'. By stretching yourself a little bit here and a bit there, eventually you will be surrounded by wonderful objects, you will have an abundance of good things in your life. This includes knowledge and experiences. If you constantly upgrade your knowledge and experiences your subconscious mind will start to look out for opportunities to do so. It will help you 'get there'.

MONEY INSIGHTS:

1. Work on your business, not just in it
2. Raise your prices
3. Improve your marketing campaign
4. Update your branding
5. Book yourself into speaking engagements
6. Set up subscriptions or payment plans
7. Align your vibration with your payment plans

GOAT

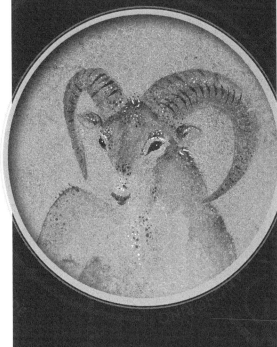

Balance, trust,
determination.

...and breathe!

GOAT

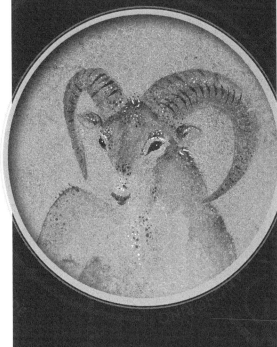

Balance, trust,
determination.

...and breathe!

34

GOAT

When we think of goat energy, we think about maintaining our balance. Much like in the ram chapter, when we start climbing the narrow ledge toward one of our tall money challenges we need to channel the sure-footed determination of our friendly goat animal.

A goat needs only the width of a two inch ledge to gain a solid foothold. Can you imagine climbing a mountain with only two inches of Mother Earth beneath your feet?

Our financial journeys can be full of treacherous paths and uphill battles. And if you want to reach for the stars, you need to trust in yourself, find your confidence and determination to reach your financial goals, the reward will certainly be worth the effort.

I would like to introduce the concept here, that we earn money through our vibration. Many money making books suggest that we earn money through our actions, which can be true to a point.

However, if you go to a networking event or speak at an event and your energetic vibration is off key then you could end up sending out 'negative vibrations' to the audience and this could affect the end result: 'no sales.'

This could sabotage the goal that your conscious mind has set up.

We each have the same 24 hours in the day, we are all living on the same planet, so why are some people doing so much better than others financially?

This can be linked to their energetic vibration. You could copy a wealthy person exactly, do everything they do, say everything they say, and yet, if your energy is not aligned to wealth you will not be as successful as they are.

They know they are going to earn more money, they believe it with every cell in their body, they have evidence that they are doing well. There is nothing in their mind that makes them doubt this.

However, if they believed that the money would not be in the bank then it would not be there.

This concept can be likened to Abraham Hicks's teachings about 'energy follows thought'

It is imperative to get and keep your vibration aligned to wealth. Keep your attention on your goals. You can 'fake it til you make it' if your energy vibration is pure, true, and aligned with your financial goals.

So how do we do this. How do we constantly ensure that our vibration is up?

In my mind, it is quite simple. When you practice lifting your vibration everyday, eventually it becomes second nature. You might think this is a hassle. And in some ways I agree with you, but think about it like this.

We have to brush our teeth every day. We have to bathe and exercise and eat to remain clean and healthy. To ensure we stay healthy. So why not include your 'energetic vibration' in the mix.

The best way to keep your energy vibration up is to practice keeping it up, as part of your daily routine. I like to do it whilst I'm brushing my teeth or grooming. Multitasking.

PHYSICAL SOLUTION

The most practical thing you can do to get your vibration up is breathe. But not just regular breathing. I want you to breath deeper than you ever have before.

Deep breathing, with your whole being.

Breathe into the deepest darkest parts of your lungs, make sure your diaphragm shifts and moves.

Breathe in for 10 counts. Then hold for 10 counts and then out for 10 counts and do this three times.

that's it. Simple?

It sounds simple, however, I was naturally a shallow breather before I started my 'money magic abundance' journey and this exercise was incredibly uncomfortable for me.

I am pleased to say it only took a week of doing this every day for me to become addicted to the wonderful feeling and benefits that followed.

Plus if I need a little top up during the day. If I'm in the office, no one even notices that I'm breathing in and holding the count for 10 counts before exhaling.

Also, if you have bad financial experience one day and it shakes your confidence then you can do the exercise quickly and easily to get back on track and on with your exciting day of making money. Following leads, ringing round to get money in, dreaming up a new marketing campaign etc.

This concept is outlined more in chapter five, see page 52, THE AXIS PRACTICE.

METAPHYSICAL SOLUTION.

The spiritual way to keep your vibrational energy up is similar to the physical one. We also breathe just as deeply and hold the breath for 10 counts before releasing.

However, you also need to think about your higher self

at this time.

Spend a moment or two imagining what your 'higher self' looks like. This tends to be the version of yourself that can be or do or have anything, this version is not limited by the constraints of this world, this version of you has access to your deepest desires, thoughts and your reason for being.

'Higher self' is a term associated with multiple belief systems, but its basic premise describes an eternal, omnipotent, conscious, and intelligent being, who is one's real self.

Blavatsky formally defined the higher self as "Atma the inseparable ray of the Universe and one self."

I have come to understand and sense that my higher self lives or exists just above my body, about half a meter above my head. My higher self tends to look similar to my actual self but with all the improvements I would make to myself if I could wave a magic wand. My 'higher selfs' hair is longer, shinier, brighter, my skin is iridescent etc.

However, along with this 'look' comes a feeling. A feeling of perfection, ultimate control, divine inspiration, an unstoppable force, all seeing and well intentioned being.

I'm very visual, so I immediately start with the look of my higher self, you might be more intellectual than I am and therefore imagine the brain of your higher self first.

It might be the biggest most intelligent brain you can imagine...

You might be very physical and think of your higher self as an athlete, with perfectly toned muscles.

It doesn't really matter how you see your 'higher self', the important thing is to imagine this part of you and imagine that as you take these four deep breaths, your 'higher self' shifts into your actual body. It moves from above your body into your body and becomes one with your physical body. The head of your 'higher self' is in line with your head, arms in line with arms legs in lines with legs etc.

After I have done this exercise I always feel incredible. I feel strong, grounded, happy, positive, energised and ready to take on the whole world.

I sometimes feel like my 'higher self' wants to escape back up outside my body. Not every day, but sometimes this happens. When it does, I imagine the energy of my higher-self has a large cloak or beautiful long jacket, with a really long trail behind it. I imagine that I take hold of this trail and tie it to the earth star chakra that sits about half a meter below my body.

I just do a simple not, imagine tying a sheet to a bed post, its not a permanent knot but it just holds my higher self in my body for the duration of the busy work day. It makes me feel sure footed and energetic at the same time.

Why do we need to do this every day and sometimes 3 or four times a day?

If you are like me, you may find that every night when you go to sleep, it seems like my 'higher self' slips off to do dreamy things, bringing me messages in dream format, after it's been off chatting with other 'higher self' beings etc.

I'm not sure exactly what mine gets up to , but I can attest to having incredibly vivid dreams. I get warnings all the time and positive beautiful messages too.

When I wake in the morning, I feel refreshed and energised but I also feel like I am a bit disconnected with my 'higher self'.

As time has gone on, and the more I have practiced the quicker I find my 'higher self' joining me for the day. And the easier it seems to achieve 'oneness'.

If you would like to know more, then read Chapter 11 'TRUTH' for further insights and examples on how to align with your higher self.

MONEY INSIGHTS:

1. Ensure your energetic vibration matches your financial abundance goals
2. Practice breathing every morning when you are getting ready for your work day
3. In challenging times, tak a moment to do the breathing exercise and get your energetic vibration back on track

EAGLE

*Power, courage,
honesty and truth.*

*From zero to hero
in one day!*

35

EAGLE

The eagle flies higher than any other bird and can spot prey from great distances.

The message from our eagle companion is to be very specific about your goals.

Be true to yourself. Take a good long hard look at yourself and your business. Be realistic with your goals and ambitions.

And really spell it out.

Example:

I mentioned to a friend that I would like to be financially independent.

She looked at me quizzically and said 'you are financially independent' ...'you run your own business' ...'you earn your own money'

I smiled then, realising I had made the mistake that so many of us make. I realised I needed to be more specific.

Yes, I do all those things, but I want to be mortgage free too. For me, I am not financially free or independent until I am living mortgage free, in the home of my dreams with savings in the bank and a steady passive income stream.

Take a moment now to think of the goals you have set and take a closer look at them and make sure they are very specific.

To help, list the goal against the following parameters: Who, what, where, how, and when.

Also break the goals down into 3 different sizes:

BIG GOAL Example, even a big goal can be quite specific:

1. WHO... 'I' or 'we' (my husband and I)
2. WHAT ...we are financially independent, living mortgage free. With savings in the bank and a passive income stream bringing money in to us every month. We live a five star life, including holidays abroad.
3. WHERE... in our gorgeous home that we have spent time and money updating to look just the way we want, filled with treasures we have collected from around the world.
4. HOW... we earn money from our branding business, and royalties from books we have sold.

5. WHEN ... 1 year from now.

Middle Goal Example 2: (a smaller but still very specific goal)

1. WHO... 'I' (myself, Katherine Tack)
2. WHAT...want to sell a million copies of my book 'abundance-magic'
3. WHERE...online, through our website and through popular online stores and at public events.
4. HOW...we will sell these books by incorporating traditional and modern marketing activities which include a weekly social media campaign, a monthly newsletter campaign. We will seek out appropriate public speaking events. And we will incorporate metaphysical energetic meditations to create a high vibrational energy around the book, to ensure it reaches the people who need it, who will treasure it, and gain great insights from it.
5. WHEN ...add your start date here

Example 3: (an even smaller, more specific goal)

1. WHO... 'I' (myself, Katherine Tack)
2. WHAT ...want to sell 20 copies of my book 'abundance-magic'
3. WHERE, online, through our website.
4. HOW...I have allocated 3 hours every morning this week to coming up with a great social media campaign and sending out the social media messages. Boosting them on face book for a small fee of £2 per day to my specific target audience. Adding these same messages to linked in and Twitter and Instagram. We will also

be making mini videos to show off the cards and grab attention online. We will also be energetically activating the book to ensure it reaches the exact target market.
5. WHEN ... today, right now ...(enter today's date).

I'm sure your goal will be quite different from mine, but whatever you do, please make sure it is very specific.

If you would like to learn more about activating the energy around a product or service, you can visit the website www.abundance-magic.co.uk/energy

By using the WHO, WHAT, WHERE, HOW AND WHEN system to define your goals, you give the universe or your subconscious brain very clear messages as to what it needs to do, how it needs to achieve the goal, when this needs to happen by.

It's important to spend time listing all your goals down in a journal or a dream diary or, if you like me, you may wish to keep them digital, and visit them as part of your everyday experience.

Some of us make the mistake of thinking big and writing down a 'way out there' goal and then when we don't achieve it, we become disheartened.

Think about how other people achieve greatness, think about how they break down their goals..

Do world famous athletes write down their ultimate goal and leave it at that?

Do you think Mozart went from zero to hero in one day?

Of course not, everyone has to set small achievable, specific goals, that they practice often and focus on every day. Sometimes twice a day.

Once I have written down the big, medium and small goal, I then transfer each of them into a two line goal that is written on something the size of a post it note and placed somewhere in my line of vision, a place that I look often, either the bathroom mirror, where I am bound to look twice a day or somewhere near my desk.

This bite size nugget is a reminder of the bigger goal that sits behind it and helps me to stay focused on my goals.

I am quite fussy about what I have in my home and around my office. If the goal doesn't look good, if it is written on a scruffy bit of paper then it won't hold my attention for very long, it might in fact have the opposite effect.

If a goal is worth setting then I think it is worth making it look good. Spend a bit of time thinking about where and how you want your goals to look. You could write them on a bit of paper and put them inside an empty vase or stick them to the back of a painting. No one else will know that your goal is there, but you will. And Every time you look up from your desk or walk into the room and see the object, you will be reminded of your goal and your subconscious mind will start to get the message. It will know where to focus it's energy to help you achieve your goals.

I suggest you read chapter 8 VISUALISATION for stronger, deeper visualisation techniques.

And the eagle card would also like you to look at Chapter 11 'TRUTH'

MONEY INSIGHTS:

1. Be specific about what you want
2. Use the WHO, WHAT, WHERE, HOW and WHEN model to define your goals
3. Connect with your TRUTH

WARTHOG

Vigilance, Courage, Truth.

The ugly truth!

36

WARTHOG

South Africans always laugh when they talk about the strange looking warthog or 'bush pig'
They say: 'only it's mother could love a baby bush pig'

I have had a few encounters with these interesting looking characters. I don't find them that ugly, actually I think they are quite cute...when they are not chasing me!

I was on a 3 wheeler motorbike driving on a private game farm, minding my own business, when a warthog decided I was an obvious threat to it's family. Even though the 3 wheeler itself was about 7 times the size of the warthog, it had absolutely no fear in its eyes when it charged at me. I, on the other hand, was petrified and turned tail and left the scene... post haste!

Courage in the face of adversity is the name of the business game.

Growing a business and financial wealth can be emotionally complicated, it has twists and turns that you could never have expected and it's important therefore to be prepared for these eventualities.

The ugly truth.

The best laid plans in the world can come undone in an instant.

One minute you are building your empire, riding the wave beautifully, selling your products and services to everyone who looks at you twice, and the next thing, the phone rings, or a social media post goes viral and you come plummeting down from 'cloud nine' into harsh reality. Or your products are returned. Or you get a bad review on social media... the list goes on!

Make sure you have some good coping strategies up your sleeve.

Female warthogs let their babies go into their burrows first, then they go into the burrow backwards, so that if anything comes into the burrow as a threat she can run out tusks first and protect her offspring. The warthogs tusks are like an elephants tusks, on their upper and lower jaws. They use these to fight and defend themselves against predators.

What emotional plans and or systems do you have in place to cope with a disaster?

One of the reasons people don't start their own

business, or launch their book or product or service, is because of the unknown. The fear of failure. What if you sell 100 books or 100 widgets and 50 get returned?

You need to be emotionally prepared for the fact that this could happen. I personally would say, CONGRATULATIONS! Well done! You have sold 50 books!

I would also say... 'find out why 50 were returned and do something about it'.

If you learn from your failures and do something about it, they are no longer called failures, you can then refer to them as 'learning opportunities'.

Do you think I haven't had a bad client review in all the years I have run my branding business?

When it happens, it feels like the end of the world. It feels like the rug has been pulled out from under you and you are no longer standing on solid ground. It feels like all the rules you knew have been changed and life is very uncomfortable indeed.

But guess what... it's a critical part of your personal journey. You should thank the client or the bad experience for showing you to your true path. Making you a 'stronger', 'better', 'a more experienced business owner'.

We are all different and therefore there are a hundred different coping strategies out there that could help you, dust yourself off and get back up on the horse.

I have had some truly awkward conversations during my career. Some were completely out of the blue and there was no way I could have predicted them, and some were, in retrospect, quite predictable. I just hadn't trusted my instincts. I got busy, distracted, missed the warning signs... and BAM! melt down!

The faster you get over these little (or sometimes big) tsunamis, the faster you will get back on track to earning your financial freedom and living your best life.

The reality is, negativity breeds negativity, so if you are constantly worrying about the conversation or situation, you might end up spiralling into deeper and deeper negativity and a negative emotional state attracts lots of problems.

Quickly as you can, identify what went wrong, talk about it, write it down. Meditate to get your vibration whole again and move on.

If you are emotionally prepared for the worst then it's much easier to move forward.

Some of the deepest cuts I have had are from close friends and family. A misplaced sentence from those nearest and dearest can cut us to the core. They may not even realise they are doing it.

I had a friend suggest once that my paintings were a bit of a waste of time. He is not my target market for this book or the paintings, but that doesn't mean it didn't sting. I walked around for 2 whole days playing the conversation over and over again. Until I remembered to deal with the meltdown. I employed the following techniques and moved swiftly on:

PHYSICAL SOLUTION:

A great mantra to say whenever you think of the tsunami or meltdown:
'I'm sorry this happened, thank you for the lesson, I forgive you and myself, I have moved on'

METAPHYSICALLY

The best meditation to get you back on track is the breathing in your higher self. Stay connected to your true self and you will start to feel grounded again. The full meditation is available at:
www.abundance-magic.co.uk/AXISPRACTICE

Please also read Chapter 11 'TRUTH' to understand what might be holding you back to achieve your abundance goals.

MONEY INSIGHTS:

1. Be prepared for tsunamis and meltdowns
2. Raise your vibration as soon as possible after any Tsunami or meltdown occurs
3. Write about it, tell someone, do what it takes to get over it and move on

Printed in Great Britain
by Amazon